Dr. Paul's
FEELING GOOD
ToolBox

100's
of Categories
1,000's
of ways to
THINK and ACT
to FEEL Great!

Dr. Paul J. Young

Dr. Paul's
FEELING GOOD TOOLBOX

How To THINK and ACT Correctly When You Are...

- **Depressed**
- **Anxious**
- **Stressed**
- **Angry**
- **Grieving**
- **Resentful**
- **Lonely**
- **Fearful**

A *FEEL GOOD* BOOK

Dr. Paul J. Young

DEDICATION: This book is dedicated to all readers who have read my DR. PAUL'S TOTAL RELIEF series and are learning how to unlock the prison doors to their depression , anxiety, stress, loneliness, fear and other emotional difficulties and are finding relief. Keep on. The best is yet to come!

This is a **DrPaulPress.com** publication

A **TOTAL RELIEF** *SYSTEMS* **publication**

All my books are written in a conversational, informal style on purpose. Formality too often bores. I don't want you to get bored while reading this book. I want you to finish it, learn from it and live the truth out in your life. My desire, more than anything, is to help you find TOTAL RELIEF from your depression.

You will find the formatting of the paragraphs and sentences are arranged differently than most other books. This makes it easy to read, easy to get the principles, and most of all will help you, my dear reader, to blast through your depression and find the joy you deserve.

Bravo!

This book is not intended to replace any kind of therapy you are presently taking. **ALWAYS TALK WITH YOUR DOCTOR OR THERAPIST BEFORE MAKING ANY RADICAL CHANGES.** And DO NOT stop taking your medication until you have worked through all my TOTAL RELIEF books and learned how to apply my unique program. Then, and only then, should you talk with your therapist or doctor to see if you can either stop or reduce your medications.

A MESSAGE FROM
DR. PAUL

My Dear Reader,

Many of you have read at least one of my TOTAL RELIEF books and have blasted through your depression, anxiety, stress, loneliness, anger, or any one of a number of difficulties you have faced. What I teach works. It is based on a proven system called Cognitive Behavioral Therapy (CBT).

COGNITIVE-BEHAVIORAL THERAPY *I believe, has been proven to be one of the best, if not the best approach to treat depression, anxiety, stress, and a host of other emotional problems.* Test after test reveals that it is on the par with medicine without the side affects. And in the long run, it is superior because people learn how to change their lives rather than rely on chemicals to change their thoughts and behavior. **Cognitive-behavioral therapy has been shown to actually change the chemistry of the brain!**

In my books, I take this further and deeper than what most of you have experienced in your therapy or what you have discovered in your reading.

This book has a unique purpose, to help you learn how to interpret any situation, any triggering event that you are blaming for your emotional difficulties. I take hundreds of happenings, events that you tend to blame for your present feelings and show you that when you change your interpretation and action, you can change your feelings.

Too often people believe that EVENTS = EMOTION. Their emotional state is the result of bad things happening to them. This kind of thinking, however, is totally wrong and will keep you bound in the prison of your emotional state, locked up and forever longing for joy and peace.

But you have learned the lie of the above formula in my book, Dr. Paul's TOTAL Relief, Depression, Book 1, and that there is another formula based on truth.

If you read the book, you will remember the formula:

EVENT + *INTERPRETATION* + *ACTION* = EMOTION

The problem is this; most of us have developed bad habits of thinking. We tend to blame the event for our emotional state rather than our interpretations and actions that rise from that event. So we seek to change the event instead of changing the way we interpret that event. Learning how to reframe our thoughts - those destructive interpretations that are causing our emotional pain and flipping them to thoughts that bring about peace and joy, is our goal.

If you have read my books (Dr. Paul's TOTAL Relief books) and worked through my workbooks, you know what I am talking about. But you may need some further help.

This book is designed to be that special aid to teach you how to reframe any situation, any triggering event, that you may be tempted to blame for your emotional pain.

How to use this book.

1. **Find the area where you are struggling.** Is it family problems, health issues, difficulties on the job, physical concerns….whatever. Find it in this specially designed Encyclopedia Of Triggering Events.

2. **Begin practicing the new way of treating your situations that have you in emotional turmoil.** Practice. Practice. Practice. Practice changing your interpretations and actions. Work at it. It will not be easy. Why? You want to BLAME your situation, that triggering event.

You may have a habit of FIXING THE BLAME INSTEAD OF FIXING THE PROBLEM. As long as you do this, you will not become emotionally healed.

Also, people often get into trouble asking WHY? instead of asking WHAT? The "why" questions will often move you to make wrong interpretations of what is happening. It is better and healthier to ask: WHAT? What can I do? What will I do? Then do it. This alleviates a lot of the emotional pain and brings hope. You move from over analysis to action. And that's a good thing!

3. **Don't give up**. You have developed bad habits of thinking.   Do you expect to change those habits

overnight? Of course not! It will take time, effort, repetition and determination to overcome poor interpretations and actions.

4. **Smile.** The fact that you purchased this book tells me that you are working on your problems. Congratulations! Your efforts will pay off big time, giving you the joy and peace you desire.

5. In this book you will see that I will at times refer to God. If you don't believe in God, don't discount this book. Nearly 90% believe in God so I am speaking to them. Even if you disagree with other parts or what I say, come up with your own interpretations and actions. This book is only illustrative. I am not trying to dictate how you think and act.

You will find, though, that when you work through all the events and situations I cover, **you will LEARN how to flip any interpretation and come up with appropriate actions.** And that's good!

I also am a big follower of Philippians 4:8-9. It is a fantastic scripture that shows us how to use cognitive behavioral therapy in a biblical way. If you don't follow the bible or have another religion, it still has some good application to you. Read it. Follow it. And you will feel better…fast!

In the book of Philippians, from a hell hole, St. Paul gives us one of the great passages in any literature on how to think and act. In fact, much of my TOTAL Relief System is based on these verses. Let me write them out for you:

*My friends, what ever is **true,** whatever is **honorable**, whatever is **just**, whatever is **p u r e ,** w h a t e v e r i s **admirable**, whatever is **kind** and **gracious**, whatever is **excellent**, whatever is **worthy of praise**...THINK ON THESE THINGS. And keep on ACTING out your faith, the way you learned from me. And the God of peace will be with you.*

Philippians 4:8-9

These two verses contain the method that is the foundation to my whole system of getting you out of your depression, anxiety, fear, loneliness, anger, etc. It is simple, to the point, and something worth meditating on for days to come.

Table Of Contents

- **Moral failure**

- **Personal failure**

As you work through each section, be creative. I may not say it the way you would. **CHANGE WHAT I WRITE. THIS BOOK IS ONLY TO BE USED AS A GUIDE, NOT AS A "BE EVERYTHING" BOOK.**

Learn from it and find peace and joy again!

TRIGGERING EVENT	INTERPRE-TATION... FLIPPING	ACTION	FEELING
HUSBAND			
Said he doesn't love me	Though he does not love me, I love myself.	Look in the mirror and smile	Hope
	He is only saying this to hurt me. He really does love me and proves it often.	Go hug him and tell him you love him.	Determined
	Though he may not love me, I have many friends who do.	Spend time with friends who love you.	Joy

	Though he does not love me, God does and proved it.	Pray. Thank God for his love.	Satisfied
	I can't force anyone to love me.	Breathe deeply and smile.	Freedom
	I am lovable	Laugh	Happy
Does not communicate often	I choose to accept what I can get and not cry about what I cannot get.	Praise him when he does talk more deeply	Supportive
	He does communicate but not with words.	I need to be better at spotting his non-verbal cues	Optimistic
	Though he does not talk much, my friends do. At least I have someone to talk with!	Spend time with friends.	Happy
TRIGGERING EVENT	**INTERPRE-TATION... FLIPPING**	**ACTION**	**FEELING**

Unfaithful	He has been unfaithful but is repentant.	Quit blaming him and accept that he wants to change.	Kind
	What he is doing is wrong and will destroy our marriage.	See a counselor, your pastor or an attorney.	Calm
	There is nothing wrong with me. I'm a beautiful woman that's he's rejecting.	Look in the mirror and tell yourself that you are awesome!	Confident
	I have made some mistakes and chased him away with my attitudes and actions.	Lay a plan to get him back. Find areas where you can praise him. Ask him to forgive you if you have neglected him.	Receptive
Angry/Temper	I deserved it.	Ask him to forgive you.	Hopeful

	I didn't deserve it. He's an angry, emotional person.	Tell him that his anger hurts you like a bullet to the heart.	Determined
	I do not accept his anger but I accept him. He has many fine qualities that overshadow his anger.	Praise him for his great qualities.	Loving
	His rage is destroying our marriage but will not destroy me.	See a counselor, your pastor or an attorney.	Resolute
Wants sex too often	I am not a sex toy but will be loving and generous with my body.	Be a giver. Be generous with your sexual times.	Peace

I would rather be wanted than not wanted.	Smile. Say: "My husband wants me."	Happy
I have been too stingy with my body and therefore he is starved for physical attention.	Surprise him. Take the initiative. Wear him out!	Satisfied
I have too often used sex as a reward rather than as a gift. I have used it to manipulate him.	Quit manipulating and be a giver without any strings attached.	Loving

	I cannot satisfy his sexual appetite. Some people love food. He loves sex. And that's OK, but I can't give him all he wants.	Talk about it without accusing and blaming. Tell him you want to satisfy him within limits. Work together on those limits and get him to agree.	Comfortable
TRIGGERING EVENT	**INTERPRE -TATION... FLIPPING**	**ACTION**	**FEELING**
Hooked on pornography	He is a good man but destroying himself with this addiction.	Talk with him. Be open to different sexual pleasures but will not be his play-toy.	Resolute

	His addiction does not mean that I am inadequate in the bedroom.	I will keep myself looking good but not compete with what he's looking at.	Confidence
	He is a sick man and needs my help.	I will talk with a counselor, my pastor and try to get help for him.	Determined
	Addictions can be mastered.	I will give him understanding and help to overcome his addiction. We will talk about ways I can help him.	Love

Worked late again	The good thing about him being a work-a-holic is that he makes good money.	My nagging is not working. I will accept that he works a lot and praise him for the time he has for me.	Peace
	His working leaves me more time for what I want to do.	I will develop a hobby to keep me busy.	Optimistic
	He works hard because he loves me and wants to provide nice things for me and the family.	I will praise him for his hard work.	Kindness
Golfing, Fishing, Hunting again	I'm so thankful that he loves the out-of-doors and is not a couch potato.	Find activities and hobbies that would be good for me to do.	Confidence

	My love for him overcomes my loneliness for him.	Share with him how much you miss him. Make it worthwhile when he is at home with your attention.	Harmony
	He is gone not because he doesn't want to be around me but because he loves the outdoors and sports.	I will learn how to play golf, fish, hunt so that I can be with my husband.	Resolute
TRIGGERING EVENT	**INTERPRE-TATION... FLIPPING**	**ACTION**	**FEELING**
Did not thank me or praise me for a good dinner I fixed.	I know I'm a great cook!	Tell him you want to fix the best meals for him. Have him grade each meal so that you can fix what he likes.	Determined

| I may not be the best in the kitchen, but at least I try. | Take some cooking lessons. Watch cooking shows on TV. Improve. Learn what he likes and fix it. Do something special at times to grab his attention. | Confidence |
| He is not the praising type but that doesn't mean he didn't like it. | Accept him for who he is. Stop trying to change him. Praise, praise, praise. Develop a culture of praise. He may catch on. | Peace |

Doesn't tell me he loves me.	He told me he loves me before. That means he still does. I should take his word for it.	Keep saying to him: "I love you," even if he doesn't respond.	Determined
	The key is not telling me but showing me that he loves me. Words are cheap.	Look for ways that SHOW you that he loves you. Compleme nt him for this.	Supportive
	Men are not always the best at communica tion.	Accept this.	Serenity
Never or rarely praises me.	I do not need his praise to know what good I do or what positive traits I have.	I will develop a list of positive traits I have and praise myself!	Confidence

TRIGGERING EVENT	INTERPRE -TATION... FLIPPING	ACTION	FEELING
	Though he doesn't praise me, I have friends and family that do!	Thank your friends and family for praising you. Tell them how good it makes you feel.	Gratitude
	He may not like me but I do!	Clap	Joy Confidence
Didn't bathe again (oogh!)	He smells but at least he's here and loves me.	Buy him some men's cologne and praise him when he uses it.	Forgiving
	I will bathe with him!	Tempt him into the shower (you know how!)	Celebration
	He has good reasons for not bathing. I'm going to find them out.	Ask him why he does not bathe often. Do it without condemnat ion.	Peace

	Just because his body stinks does not mean he stinks personally.	Encourage him to bathe. Let him know that others are beginning to talk about the way he smells.	Courage
Lazy	I would rather him be lazy and lay around the house than too busy.	Plan projects to do TOGETHER.	Resolute
	He is sure good at being relaxed!	Relax with him. Don't nag.	Peace
	There is no harm done with his laziness.	Quit blaming him and trying to change him	Freedom

Stingy	He has a tight grip on our money. That's far better than spending all we have and putting us in the poor house!	Learn how to give generously to yourself.	Supportive
	I will show how to give without wasting money.	Give him things he needs and wants with money you have saved.	Supportive
	He may be fearful of losing what we have. That's a good fear and I will respect that.	Encourage him to enjoy the NOW as he plans for the future.	Kind
Drives too fast	He hates to waste time.	Stop nagging and relax.	Peace

	He hates being late. That's a good quality.	Praise him for always being on time. Encourage him to leave a little earlier so he won't have to rush.	Encouraged
	He loves going fast. This goes along with his personality that likes to get things done quickly. Because of this he's a great success.	Accept him for who he is. Admire him. Don't focus on the areas you want to change but on the things you like about him.	Confidence
I caught him lying again	He lies because he is afraid of telling me the truth. I need to make it safe for him to be honest… always.	Lovingly talk with him about his lying. Affirm him and let him know that telling the truth is safe with you.	Peace

TRIGGERING EVENT	INTERPRE-TATION… FLIPPING	ACTION	FEELING
	He has a habit of lying. That's not good. But he wants to change. That's great!	I will lovingly help him to tell the truth… always.	Encouraged
	Lying is better than being unfaithful, being abusive and hateful.	I will focus on his good traits and not on his bad.	Hope
	Yes, he lies. But he still loves me.	Affirm him and tell him how much you love him. Show it by deeds.	Courage

Critical statements about me	He is so critical of me because he is critical of himself.	I will help him to be more accepting of himself by praising him. If I model this he might do that for me.	Hope
	I hate to be criticized but I love him!	Go hug him. Smile.	Happy
	I need to learn how to be more critical in a helpful way.	Study the subject of HELPFUL criticism. How can you do it in a way that will build and not destroy?	Resolute
Rage, hits me	I don't deserve this. It's his fault.	Call 911. He must be held accountabl e	Resolute

	I love him but hate his physical abuse.	I will get him the help he needs to get to the bottom of WHY he is so abusive.	Peace
He's fat and can't stop eating when he should	He really enjoys life. I like that!	Focus on his love of life and his positive traits.	Peace
	Fat is beautiful!	Quit blaming him and praise him.	Joy
	Instead of blaming him I should take responsibility for myself - the way I cook for him.	Cook meals that will satisfy him but be less calories.	Content
TRIGGERING EVENT	**INTERPRE-TATION... FLIPPING**	**ACTION**	**FEELING**

	If I truly love him, I will help him to eat less.	Talk about his eating in a non-judgmental way. Help him to come up with a plan for eating less.	Supportive
	He stuffs his food because we are always in a rush.	Slow down. Smell the roses (the food). Savor it. Put your fork down after each bite. Wait.	Satisfied
Got drunk	It was a stupid mistake. He will learn from it.	Don't be an enabler.	Resolute

This is happening too often. I will get help for him.	Help your husband to see that he may have a brain problem. Alcohol may be acting like morphine to the brain.	Determined
His getting drunk and spurning my help and insight means that I may have to help him decide between the bottle or me.	Give your husband an ultimatum - stop his destructive behavior or the marriage will cease. Tell him you want him to get help - now (join AA, etc.)	Courageous
His choosing the bottle does not mean I'm not a worthwhile person.	Praise yourself. Don't get caught up in blaming yourself. Smile.	Peace

TRIGGERING EVENT	INTERPRE-TATION... FLIPPING	ACTION	FEELING
	Yes. He loves to drink. He also loves me too.	Help his love for you to conquer his bad drinking habits.	Gentle
Domineering, dictatorial	He loves being in charge. And he's usually right about his choices, just overbearing in the way he does it.	I will not get into an ego battle with him. I will pick my battles carefully and let him win when it's not really that important.	Calm
	Both of us can't have our way. Most of the decisions he makes are good. It's not worth the friction to fight for what I want.	Breath. Relax. I don't always have to have it my way.	Peace

	He dictates because he loves me and wants the best for me. And he really believes his decisions are best for both of us.	I need to thank him for his determination to lead us. I will, at times, help him to understand my point of view if it is the right time.	Gratitude
Vindictive, abusive	This type of anger is not acceptable. I love myself too much to continue to put up with this.	You must tell him that this kind of behavior cannot continue or you will end the relationship. Affirm your love for him and encourage him to get help.	Resolution
	He is this way because his father was this way.	Help your husband to get into counseling to work on his anger.	Strong

	I choose to not let his words wound me.	Draw up a list of positive traits about yourself. Recite them to yourself.	Calm
Flirts with another woman	Yes he flirts, but he is faithful to me.	Have a discussion with him as to why he flirts. Listen. Don't judge. Thank him for his faithfulness.	Happy
	Say: "Look at the way other women notice my husband and flirt with him. They wish they had him, BUT I DO!"	Clap. Be thankful.	Cheer

TRIGGERING EVENT	INTERPRE-TATION... FLIPPING	ACTION	FEELING
Forgot your birthday, anniversary, Valentines Day, Mother's Day	Dates don't mean much to him, but I do. He tells me that he loves me and that is enough.	Accept him for who he is. Admire him. Don't focus on the areas you want to change but on the things you like about him.	Peace
	Yes, I would love to be noticed more, but he does work hard for us and is faithful to me.	Take what you can get not what you don't get. It is not a sin to forget dates! Let it go.	Joy
	Though he forgets these dates, I will remember them and give him a card.	Don't do tit for tat. Be loving and kind always, not expecting anything in return.	Satisfied

Hooked on drugs	I may be able to blame him for starting but I can't blame him for not stopping. He is addicted and needs help.	Pray. Seek counsel. Talk with your pastor. Support your husband as you encourage him to deal with this addiction.	Aware
	He chooses drugs over me only because he is addicted. He is not rejecting me.	Be gentle. Use tough love when needed.	Resolute
He's a jerk!	Though he's a jerk, I will still love him and seek his best.	Write out 20 positive traits for him and share them with him.	Caring
	Just because I married a jerk does not mean I'm one.	Counter his jerkiness with love.	Brave

TRIGGERING EVENT	INTERPRE-TATION... FLIPPING	ACTION	FEELING
	I cannot change him but I can change my circumstances.	Spend time with girlfriends.	Anticipation
	I choose not to go berserk over the jerk!	Smile, laugh, dance	Joy

TRIGGERING EVENT	INTERPRE-TATION... FLIPPING	ACTION	FEELING
WIFE			
Said she doesn't love me	Though she does not love me, I love myself.	Look in the mirror and smile	Hope
	She is only saying this to hurt me. She really does love me and proves it often.	Go hug her and tell her you love her.	Determined

	Though she may not love me, I have many friends who do.	Spend time with friends who love you.	Joy
	Though she does not love me, God does and proved it.	Pray. Thank God for his love.	Satisfied
	I can't force anyone to love me.	Breathe deeply and smile.	Freedom
	I am lovable	Laugh	Happy
Talks too much	I really married a vivacious person!	Smile. Determine not to blame.	Satisfied
	She talks so much because I don't.	I will learn how to talk more and be more open in my conversations.	Resolute

TRIGGERING EVENT	INTERPRETATION... FLIPPING	ACTION	FEELING
	She speaks a lot from her head and not from her heart. Why?	I will model speaking from my heart and encourage her to do the same.	Satisfied
Does not communicate often	I choose to accept what I can get and not cry about what I cannot.	Praise her when she does talk more deeply	Supportive
	She does communicate but not with words.	I need to be better at spotting her non-verbal cues	Optimistic
TRIGGERING EVENT	**INTERPRE-TATION... FLIPPING**	**ACTION**	**FEELING**
	Though she does not talk much, my friends do. At least I have someone to talk with!	Spend time with friends.	Happy

Unfaithful	She has been unfaithful but is repentant.	Quit blaming her and accept that she wants to change.	Kind
	What she is doing is wrong and will destroy our marriage.	See a counselor, your pastor or an attorney.	Calm
	There is nothing wrong with me. I'm a handsome man that she is rejecting.	Look in the mirror and tell yourself that you are awesome!	Confident
	I have made some mistakes and chased her away with my attitudes and actions.	Lay a plan to get her back. Find areas where you can praise her. Ask her to forgive you if you have neglected her.	Receptive
Angry/Temper	I deserved it.	Ask her to forgive you.	Hopeful

	I didn't deserve it. She's an angry, emotional person.	Tell her that her anger hurts you like a bullet to the heart.	Determined
	I do not accept her anger but I accept her. She has many fine qualities that overshadow her anger.	Praise her for her great qualities.	Loving
	Her rage is destroying our marriage but will not destroy me.	See a counselor, your pastor or an attorney.	Resolute
Cries all the time	I hate her crying but I love her.	Put your arm around her. Empathize.	Understand
	She is depressed.	I will get her help.	Resolute

Critical, fault-finding	Her mother was the same way. I can't blame my wife because of this.	I will not get caught up in blaming (blame for blame) but instead praise her.	Determined
TRIGGERING EVENT	**INTERPRE-TATION... FLIPPING**	**ACTION**	**FEELING**
	It stings when she criticizes me. Yet she is often right, I just don't like to admit it.	Accept the criticism with a smile. Tell her "thanks." This will shock her and possibly make her less critical.	Peace

	She blames me because she too often blames herself. This self criticism leads to criticism of others.	She needs much more praise from me than criticism. I will draw up a list of 100 positive characteristics she has and things she does.	Loving
	Her criticisms are only jabs, not knock-out punches.	Go with the flow.	Relaxed
Doesn't want sex very often	At least she allows for some time in the bedroom.	Focus on her personal traits instead of her body.	Understand
	I did not marry her for her body but for WHO she is.	Praise her for WHO she is.	Confidence

	She is not comfortable with her body, the way she looks.	I will try to help her feel comfortable with the way she looks, and praise her appropriately.	Loving
	She's just shy.	Be patient. In time she will overcome this shyness.	Patience
Worked late again	The good thing about her being a work-a-holic is that she makes good money.	My nagging is not working. I will accept that she works a lot and praise her for the time she has for me.	Peace
	Her working leaves me more time for what I want to do.	I will develop a hobby to keep me busy.	Optimistic

	She works hard because she loves me and want to provide nice things for our family.	I will praise her for her hard work.	Kindness
Dirty. Doesn't keep a clean house	This is her basic job, to take care of the family including our house. Maybe she isn't challenged enough.	Find out what challenges her and move her in that direction.	Sincerity
	Who likes to clean house!	Get a maid.	Peace
TRIGGERING EVENT	**INTERPRE-TATION... FLIPPING**	**ACTION**	**FEELING**

	Her lack of initiative means that she does not feel good about herself. A dirty home may point to low self-esteem.	Don't fix the blame but fix the problem. Help her see a counselor, or your pastor who can help her feel better about herself.	Resolute
Spends too much money. Always shopping.	Shopping makes her feel good and I want her to feel good.	I need to help her find other ways to feel good besides shopping.	Less anxiety
	She can't fill her heart's need with things.	I will help her focus on what she REALLY wants.	Caring
	She is helping the economy!	Smile.	Optimistic

	She doesn't understand that in time we will be hurt financially.	Sit down. Plan a budget. Let her be part of making the decisions. Allow plenty for her.	Hopeful
Doesn't tell me she loves me.	She told be she loves me before. That means she still does. I should take her word for it.	Keep saying to her: "I love you," even if she doesn't respond.	Determined
	The key is not telling me but showing me that she loves me. Words are cheap.	Look for ways that SHOW you that she loves you. Complement her for this.	Supportive
	Some women are not always the best at communication.	Accept this.	Serenity

Never or rarely praises me.	I do not need her praise to know what good I do or what positive traits I have.	I will develop a list of positive traits I have and praise myself!	Confidence
	Though she doesn't praise me, I have friends and family that do!	Thank your friends and family for praising you. Tell them how good it makes you feel.	Gratitude
	She may not like me but I do!	Clap	Joy Confidence
TRIGGERING EVENT	**INTERPRE-TATION... FLIPPING**	**ACTION**	**FEELING**
Didn't bathe again (oogh!)	She smells but at least she is here and loves me.	Buy her some women's cologne and praise her when she uses it.	Forgiving

	I will bathe with her!	Tempt her into the shower (you know how!)	Celebration
	She has good reasons for not bathing. I'm going to find them out.	Ask her why she does not bathe often. Do it without condemnation.	Peace
	Just because her body stinks does not mean she stinks personally.	Encourage her to bathe. Let her know that others are beginning to talk about the way she smells.	Courage
Lazy	I would rather her be lazy and lay around the house than too busy.	Plan projects to do TOGETHER.	Resolute
	She is sure good at Relaxing!	Relax with her. Don't nag.	Peace

	There is no harm done with her laziness.	Quit blaming her and trying to change her.	Freedom
Stingy	She has a tight grip on our money. That's far better than spending all we have and putting us in the poor house!	Learn how to give generously to yourself.	Supportive
	I will show how how to give without wasting money.	Give her things she needs and wants with money you have saved.	Supportive
	She may be fearful of losing what we have. That's a good fear and I will respect that.	Encourage her to enjoy the NOW as she plans for the future.	Kind

Drives too fast	She hates to waste time.	Stop nagging and relax.	Peace
TRIGGERING EVENT	**INTERPRE -TATION… FLIPPING**	**ACTION**	**FEELING**
	She hates being late. That's a good quality.	Praise her for always being on time. Encourage her to leave a little earlier so she won't have to rush.	Encouraged
	She loves going fast. This goes along with her personality that likes to get things done quickly. Because of this she's a great success.	Accept her for who she is. Admire her. Don't focus on the areas you want to change but on the things you like about her.	Confidence

I caught her lying again	She lies because she is afraid of telling me the truth. I need to make it safe for her to be honest… always.	Lovingly talk with her about her lying. Affirm her and let her know that telling the truth is safe with you.	Peace
	She has a habit of lying. That's not good. But she wants to change. That's great!	I will lovingly help her to tell the truth… always.	Encouraged
	Lying is better than being unfaithful, being abusive and hateful.	I will focus on her good traits and not on her bad.	Hope
	Yes, she lies. But she still loves me.	Affirm her and tell her how much you love her. Show it by deeds.	Courage

TRIGGERING EVENT	INTERPRETATION... FLIPPING	ACTION	FEELING
Critical statements about me	She is so critical of me because she is critical of herself.	I will help her to be more accepting of herself by praising her. If I model this she might do that for me.	Hope
	I hate to be criticized but I love her!	Go hug her. Smile.	Happy
	I need to learn how to be more critical in a helpful way.	Study the subject of HELPFUL criticism. How can you do it in a way that will build and not destroy?	Resolute
She's fat and can't stop eating when she should	She really enjoys life. I like that!	Focus on her love of life and her positive traits.	Peace

	Fat is beautiful!	Quit blaming her and praise her.	Joy
	Instead of blaming her, I will take responsibility for myself - the way I encourage her to cook for me.	Encourage her to cook meals that will satisfy both of you but have less calories.	Content
	If I truly love her, I will help her to eat less.	Talk about her eating in a non-judgmental way. Help her to come up with a plan for eating less.	Supportive

	She stuffs her food because we are always in a rush.	Slow down. Smell the roses (the food). Savor it. Put your fork down after each bite. Model how to Wait.	Satisfied
Got drunk	It was a stupid mistake. She will learn from it.	Don't be an enabler.	Resolute
	This is happening too often. I will get help for her.	Help your wife to see that she may have a brain problem. Alcohol may be acting like morphine to her brain.	Determined

Her getting drunk and spurning my help and insight means that I may have to help her decide between the bottle or me.	Give you wife an ultimatum - stop her destructive behavior or the marriage will cease. Tell her you want her to get help - NOW (join AA, etc.)	Courageous
Her choosing the bottle does not mean I'm not a worthwhile person.	Praise yourself. Don't get caught up in blaming yourself. Smile.	Peace
Yes. She loves to drink. She also loves me too.	Help her love for you to conquer her bad drinking habits.	Gentle

Domineering, dictatorial	She loves being in charge. And she's usually right about her choices, just overbearing in the way she does it.	I will not get into an ego battle with her. I will pick my battles carefully and let her win when it's not really that important.	Calm
TRIGGERING EVENT	**INTERPRE-TATION... FLIPPING**	**ACTION**	**FEELING**
	Both of us can't have our way. Most of the decisions she makes are good. It's not worth the friction to fight for what I want.	Breath. Relax. I don't always have to have it my way.	Peace

	She dictates because she loves me and wants the best for me. And she really believes her decisions are best for both of us.	I need to thank her for her determination to lead us. I will, at times, help her to understand my point of view if it is the right time.	Gratitude
Vindictive, abusive	This type of anger is not acceptable. I love myself too much to continue to put up with this.	You must tell her that this kind of behavior cannot continue or you will end the relationship. Affirm your love for her and encourage her to get help.	Resolution
	She is this way because his father was this way.	Help your wife to get into counseling to work on her anger.	Strong

	I choose to not let her words wound me.	Draw up a list of positive traits about yourself. Recite them to yourself.	Calm
Flirts with another man	Yes she flirts, but she is faithful to me.	Have a discussion with her as to why she flirts. Listen. Don't judge. Thank her for her faithfulness.	Happy
	Say: "Look at the way other men notice my wife and flirt with her. They wish they had her, BUT I DO!"	Clap. Be thankful.	Cheer

Forgot your birthday, anniversary, Valentines Day, Father's Day	Dates don't mean much to her, but I do. She tells me that she loves me and that is enough.	Accept her for who she is. Admire her. Don't focus on the areas you want to change but on the things you like about her.	Peace
	Yes, I would love to be noticed more, but she does work hard for us and is faithful to me	Take what you can get not what you won't get. It is not a sin to forget dates! Let it go.	Joy
	Though she forgets these dates, I will remember them and send a card.	Don't do tit for tat. Be loving and kind always, not expecting anything in return.	Satisfied
TRIGGERING EVENT	**INTERPRE -TATION... FLIPPING**	**ACTION**	**FEELING**

Hooked on drugs	I may be able to blame her for starting but I can't blame her for not stopping. She is addicted and needs help.	Pray. Seek counsel. Talk with your pastor. Support your wife as you encourage her to deal with this addiction.	Aware
	She chooses drugs over me only because she is addicted. She is not rejecting me.	Be gentle. Use tough love when needed.	Resolute
They's a jerk!	Though she's a jerk, I will still love her and seek her best.	Write out 20 positive traits for her and share them with her.	Caring
	Just because I married a jerk does not mean I'm one.	Counter her jerkiness with love.	Brave

	I cannot change her but I can change my circumstances.	Spend time with male friends.	Anticipation
	I choose not to go berserk over the jerk!	Smile, laugh, dance	Joy
Doesn't take pride in her looks	I choose to love her no matter how she looks.	Relax. Looks aren't everything.	Peace
	Her lack of pride shows her lack of Inner confidence	Spend time thinking how to build her inner confidence. Read. Go to a counselor or pastor and get help.	Supportive
	Wow! If only she would take more time, she would be a knock-out.	Surprise her by a makeover at a spa.	Bold

Overly accommodating	She loves to please, and that's good!	Praise her. Yet tell her that you love her so much you hate seeing other people take advantage of her.	Supportive
	She is afraid to say: "No." Why? Where is the fear coming from? I will help her find out.	Find a good book on how to say: "No," a book that will help her to be more assertive.	Determined
	She is so easy to live with, and I like that.	Do not take advantage of her accommodating spirit.	Pleasure
TRIGGERING EVENT	**INTERPRE-TATION... FLIPPING**	**ACTION**	**FEELING**
CHILDREN			

Fighting	This is not unusual. After all, they are children!	I will help them to learn to be givers and not takers and thus reduce much of the fighting.	Peace
	One of my children needs special attention. That's the reason they are picking on the other child.	Give special attention to them. Help them to FEEL accepted.	Resolute
Fighting	The children want MY attention. I have neglected them and thus they are telling me that through their fighting.	Set aside special time for THEM. Go to the park, take them out for a special treat, play a game with them.	Loving

	I have been too lenient when they fight. I need to have consequences.	Set up a penalty and reward system. Have them help you do this. When they fight they get penalized. When they have a day of peace they get rewarded.	Confidence
Sick	Young children need to see the doctor 4 or 5 times a year. So this is normal.	Relax. Smile. Your children are normal.	Acceptance
	Though getting up in the middle of the night is a pain, my children are worth it all.	Quit complaining and embrace the happiness of raising children.	Joy

	They need immediate, emergency attention, and I will rush them to the hospital where they can hopefully get help.	Take deep breaths. Pray. Thank God that he is with you and will help.	Brave
Failure in school	Failing in school does not mean they are a failure.	Quit fixing the blame and fix the problem.	Resolute
	They may be trying to get attention.	Spend more time with them, listening, helping, Understand.	Gentle
	The problem could be a number of things: The school, the teacher, other children, myself, or my child.	Get some counseling. Look at the possibilities and move intelligently toward a solution.	Smart

TRIGGERING EVENT	INTERPRE-TATION… FLIPPING	ACTION	FEELING
	I need to get my child tested to make sure I am not pushing him too hard.	Work with principle or trained therapist. Find results.	Care
	They are failing because of problems in our home.	Get help. Fix the problems. Fix yourself!	Bold
Won't clean room	My nagging is not working.	Develop a reward system - positive and negative. Grade the room each day. They get money if they do well and money subtracted if they don't. Pay each week.	Satisfied

	It's their room, not mine.	Quit nagging and close the door.	Peace
	Carrying out their responsibilities results in privileges.	Sit down with them and have them help you draw up a list of privileges if they keep their room clean and picked up.	Confident
Disobedient	It is my responsibility to help them learn how to obey.	Help children to know WHY they need to obey.	Optimistic
	The rebellious behavior is normal, but must come to an end.	Draw up a list of PAINFUL results for rebellious behavior. Make sure they understand that intentional rebellion will be painful for them.	Resolute

Disobedience is a mark of immaturity. And does it surprise me that they disobey since they are but children?	ACCEPT they are children. Smile. ACCEPT too your responsibility to help them to grow up.	Acceptance
This gives me a chance to help them to learn how to be a better person.	Use disobedient behavior as a teaching tool. In one since their disobedience becomes a POSITIVE time for you to help them to grow into the person they should become.	Encouraged

Lie	They are fearful of being caught. And that's good!	Set up positive/ negative reward system for lying. Make it worthwhile for them to tell the truth.	Optimistic
	They don't understand why lying is wrong and hurtful not just to others but to them.	Explain to them the consequen ces of lying. Relax. If you do, lovingly they will learn.	Relaxed
TRIGGERING EVENT	**INTERPRE -TATION... FLIPPING**	**ACTION**	**FEELING**
Mean, bully	They are trying to feel important.	Draw up a list of positive traits about them. Help them to embrace these.	Loving

	They fight and bully because they don't see the rewards that come from being nice.	Help them to see the difference between being a GIVER and a TAKER. Givers are the ultimate winners in life.	Understand
	He's mean but I still love him!	Smile. Keep loving. Hug him.	Peace
Boyfriend, girlfriend problems	This is normal.	Draw up some directions TOGETHER.	Cooperative
	Their hormones are working. That's good.	Help them understand what's happening and how to be successful with the opposite sex.	Empathy

	Sexual involvement is natural but not good until married.	Talk openly about sexual involvement discussing options. Lead them in a commitment to wait.	Hopeful
	Living together.	Love. Be firm with your convictions. Accept WHO they are not WHAT they are doing (if this is in line with your moral convictions)	Friendly
Daughter gets pregnant	They made a wrong choice but we can make some good choices for her and the baby.	Smile. Help her look at the options.	Compassion

| | This is not the end of the world. In a few years the mistake will be forgotten and we will be joyful in this new gift of life! | Forgive. Don't fix the blame but fix the problem. Work together to do it. | Confident |
| Drinking before age 21 | This is not good, but it's not the the worst thing that can happen. Most children experiment at this age. | Relax. Breathe. Guide. Have a good, open talk. Accept who they are, not what they did. | Peace |

	Though this is normal at this age, it is a wake up call to step in and help.	Show love and concern. Ask: Where did they get the drinks, who were they with, describe how did it feel? Make this a learning situation.	Acceptance
Drug involvement	Thank God I discovered their involvement!	Don't panic. Breathe. Develop a plan to help.	Resolution
	Their drug involvement is not good. My discovery is.	Pray. Get counsel from your pastor or counselor. Read. Plan. Be positive. Your attitude will be a great help.	Positive
TRIGGERING EVENT	**INTERPRE-TATION... FLIPPING**	**ACTION**	**FEELING**

	Though they are hooked, I can get them help.	Find a place to take them for help. Don't condemn. Love. It may take tough love to pull them through.	Compassion
Rebellion	This opens my eyes to the fact that I must take stronger action. And I will!	Lead. Show tough love. Draw up a list of things that must change. Be courageous. Praise, then discipline, then praise.	Passion

	I need to make sure that I am not creating this resistance by the way I act and lead.	Have an open conversation with your child. Find out what they really want. Help them develop a plan to get it.	Sincere
Shy, withdrawn	This is not necessarily a bad thing.	Accept that they have a quiet personality	Peace
	They may be struggling with inferiority.	Help them to see their strengths and to move ahead in these areas Praise them.	Satisfied
Grumpy	It could be that they always seem tired and this grumpiness is the result.	Sit down with them and develop a schedule. Let them take leadership.	Tender

	I need to become more aware about sleeping habits, eating, and be aware that they might be on drugs.	This is a time for me to wake up and pay attention. You are the parent. Be one. Be involved.	Hopeful
Lazy	I need to find what motivates them.	Draw up with them a reward system that would motivate them.	Joy
	Part of it is my problem. I was too uninvolved in their lives and let this habit get rooted.	Be aware. Be not afraid to confront, lovingly. Be confident.	Hope
TRIGGERING EVENT	**INTERPRE -TATION... FLIPPING**	**ACTION**	**FEELING**

FATHER			
Not loving	He loves me but has a hard time showing it.	Write out reasons why your father loves you. Smile.	Pleased
	He tends to be selfish. To bad for him. He is missing out on loving me.	Pump your fist. Say: "I am worth loving."	Confidence
	Though he struggles with showing love, he is a great dad.	List all the reasons your father is a great dad.	Satisfied
Abusive	This is wrong what he is doing, but I will not let it control how I feel.	Talk with a counselor or a pastor	Resolute

	I hate his abusiveness but I love him.	List his good qualities. Don't let his abuse hide what is good about him.	Peace
	I love him too much to let him continue on this path.	Lovingly confront. Use the sandwich method: Praise, Confront, Praise.	Tenacious
Controlling, domineering	I choose not to fight this characteristic but to love and accept him.	Show love to him often.	Loving
	He is afraid of losing control.	Learn ways to help him face his fears. Read. Talk with a counselor about this.	Empathetic

	I hate it when he tries to control me, but I choose not to give into hate but to love him completely.	List ways you can show love.	Honesty
	I resist his control because I like to be in control. I am a lot like him, no wonder we collide.	Accept your role in the tug-a-war for control. Breathe. It's OK. You are normal.	Peace
Absent	My absent father does not mean that I am worthless.	Draw up a list of reasons why you are a good person.	Confident
	I can be happy even if he is gone.	List reasons why you can be happy.	Joyful

	He is absent because he is providing for us. We have a beautiful home, great food, and many other things because of his work.	Don't focus on his absence but on the gifts his absence produce.	Content
TRIGGERING EVENT	**INTERPRE -TATION... FLIPPING**	**ACTION**	**FEELING**
	His continual absence is not good for him or me. Yet I believe that many good things come from what seems not good.	List some good things that could come from his absence. What are some things you can learn from it?	Hope
Alcohol, drug addiction	He is a very sick man.	Encourage him to get help.	Empathy

	No matter how many times he fails, I will love him. After all, he's family!	Constantly surround him with your love.	Supportive
	I love him too much to let him continue on in his destructive path.	Do an intervention.	Resolute
	This behavior is not against me, but is against himself.	Go to Al-Anon to find help.	Understand
	I cannot change him. He must change himself.	Quit manipulating and keep encouraging.	Peace
Rage, hits me	I don't deserve this. It's his fault.	Call 911. He must be held accountable.	Resolute

	I love him but hate his physical abuse.	I will get him the help he needs to get to the bottom of WHY he is so abusive.	Peace
Doesn't tell me he loves me.	He told me he loves me before. That means he still does. I should take his word for it.	Keep saying to him: "I love you," even if he doesn't respond.	Determined
	The key is not telling me but showing me that he loves me. Words are cheap.	Look for ways that SHOW you that he loves you. Compliment him for this.	Supportive
	Men are not always the best at communication.	Accept this.	Serenity

Never or rarely praises me.	I do not need his praise to know what good I do or what positive traits I have.	I will develop a list of positive traits I have and praise myself!	Confidence
	Though he doesn't praise me, I have friends and family that do!	Thank your friends and family for praising you. Tell them how good it makes you feel.	Gratitude
	He may not like me but I do!	Clap	Joy Confidence
TRIGGERING EVENT	**INTERPRE-TATION... FLIPPING**	**ACTION**	**FEELING**
Angry/Temper	I deserved it.	Ask him to forgive you.	Hopeful
	I didn't deserve it. He's an angry, emotional person.	Tell him that his anger hurts you like a bullet to the heart.	Determined

	I do not accept his anger but I accept him. He has many fine qualities that overshadow his anger.	Praise him for his great qualities.	Loving
	His rage is destroying our relationship but will not destroy me.	See a counselor, your pastor.	Resolute
Critical statements about me	He is so critical of me because he is critical of himself.	I will help him to be more accepting of himself by praising him. If I model this he might do that for me.	Hope
	I hate to be criticized but I love him!	Go hug him. Smile.	Happy

	I need to learn how to be more critical in a helpful way.	Study the subject of HELPFUL criticism. How can you do it in a way that will build and not destroy?	Resolute
Stingy	He has a tight grip on our money. That's far better than spending all we have and putting us in the poor house!	Learn how to give generously to yourself.	Supportive
	I will show how how to give without wasting money.	Give him things he needs and wants with money you have saved.	Supportive

TRIGGERING EVENT	INTERPRETATION... FLIPPING	ACTION	FEELING
	He may be fearful of losing what we have. That's a good fear and I will respect that.	Encourage him to enjoy the NOW as he plans for the future.	Kind
He's a jerk!	Though he's a jerk, I will still love him and seek his best.	Write out 20 positive traits for him and share them with him.	Caring
	Just because my dad's a jerk does not mean I'm one.	Counter his jerkiness with love.	Brave
	I cannot change him but I can change my circumstances.	Spend time with friends.	Anticipation
	I choose not to go berserk over the jerk!	Smile, laugh, dance	Joy

Hooked on pornography	He is a good man but destroying himself with this addiction.	Talk with him. about his destructive behavior.	Resolute
	He is a sick man and needs my help.	I will talk with a counselor, my pastor and try to get help for him.	Determined
	Addictions can be mastered.	I will give him understanding and help to overcome his addiction. We will talk about ways I can help him.	Love
Unfaithful to my mother	Somehow he can have sex with one woman but still love mom. Thank God he still does.	Focus on his love not on his unfaithfulness.	Peace

What he is doing is wrong. I don't accept this failure but I do accept him.	Draw up a list of positive traits about your father. Repeat them to yourself and to him at times. Focus on the good and not the bad.	Serenity
My mother does not like his unfaithfulne ss but she loves him. I will follow her example.	Love uncond/tio nally.	Love
I choose to be faithful like my mother and embrace her attitudes.	Commit to being faithful in all you do.	Resolution

Does not communicate often	I choose to accept what I can get and not cry about what I cannot.	Praise him when he does talk more deeply	Supportive
	He does communicate but not with words.	I need to be better at spotting his non-verbal cues	Optimistic
	Though he does not talk much, my friends do. At least I have someone to talk with!	Spend time with friends.	Happy

TRIGGERING EVENT	INTERPRE-TATION... FLIPPING	ACTION	FEELING
MOTHER			
Not loving	She loves me but has a hard time showing it.	Write out reasons why your mother loves you. Smile.	Pleased

	She tends to be selfish and too bad for her. She is missing out on loving me.	Pump your fist. Say: "I am worth loving."	Confidence
	Though she struggles with showing love, she is a great mom.	List all the reasons your mother is a great mom.	Satisfied
Abusive	This is wrong what she is doing, but I will not let it control how I feel.	Talk with a counselor or a pastor	Resolute
	I hate her abusiveness but I love her.	List her good qualities. Don't let her abuse hide what is good about her.	Peace

	I love her too much to let her continue on this path.	Lovingly confront. Use the sandwich method: Praise, Confront, Praise.	Tenacious
Controlling, domineering	I choose not to fight this characteristic but to love and accept her.	Show love to her often.	Loving
	She is afraid of losing control.	Learn ways to help her face her fears. Read. Talk with a counselor about this.	Empathetic
	I hate it when she tries to control me, but I choose not to give into hate but to love her completely.	List ways you can show love.	Honesty

	I resist her control because I like to be in control. I am a lot like her. No wonder we collide.	Accept your role in the tug-a-war for control. Breathe. It's OK. You are normal.	Peace
Absent	My absent mother does not mean that I am worthless.	Draw up a list of reasons why you are a good person.	Confident
	I can be happy even if she is gone.	List reasons why you can be happy.	Joyful
	She is absent because she is providing for us. We have a beautiful home, great food, and many other things because of her work.	Don't focus on her absence but on the gifts her absence produce.	Content

TRIGGERING EVENT	INTERPRE-TATION... FLIPPING	ACTION	FEELING
	Her continual absence is not good for her or me. Yet I believe that many good things come from what seems not good.	List some good things that could come from her absence. What are some things you can learn from it?	Hope
Alcohol, drug addiction	She is a very sick woman.	Encourage her to get help.	Empathy
	No matter how many times she fails, I will love her. After all, she's family!	Constantly surround her with your love.	Supportive
	I love her too much to let her continue on in her destructive path.	Do an intervention.	Resolute

	This behavior is not against me, but is against herself.	Go to Al-Anon to find help.	Understand
	I cannot change her. She must change herself.	Quit manipulating and keep encouraging.	Peace
Rage, hits me	I don't deserve this. It's her fault.	Call 911. She must be held accountable	Resolute
	I love her but hate her physical abuse.	I will get her the help she needs to get to the bottom of WHY she is so abusive.	Peace

Doesn't tell me she loves me.	She told me she loves me before. That means she still does. I should take her word for it.	Keep saying to her: "I love you," even if she doesn't respond.	Determined
	The key is not telling me but showing me that she loves me. Words are cheap.	Look for ways that SHOW you that she loves you. Compleme nt her for this.	Supportive
	People are not always the best at communica tion.	Accept this.	Serenity
Never or rarely praises me.	I do not need her praise to know what good I do or what positive traits I have.	I will develop a list of positive traits I have and praise myself!	Confidence

	Though she doesn't praise me, I have friends and family that do!	Thank your friends and family for praising you. Tell them how good it makes you feel.	Gratitude
	She may not like me but I do!	Clap	Joy Confidence
Angry/Temper	I deserved it.	Ask her to forgive you.	Hopeful
	I didn't deserve it. She's an angry, emotional person.	Tell her that her anger hurts you like a bullet to the heart.	Determined
TRIGGERING EVENT	**INTERPRE-TATION… FLIPPING**	**ACTION**	**FEELING**
	I do not accept her anger but I accept her. She has many fine qualities that overshadow her anger.	Praise her for her great qualities.	Loving

	Her rage is destroying our relationship but will not destroy me.	See a counselor, your pastor.	Resolute
Critical statements about me	She is so critical of me because she is critical of herself.	I will help her to be more accepting of herself by praising her. If I model this she might do that for me.	Hope
	I hate to be criticized but I love her!	Go hug her. Smile.	Happy
	I need to learn how to be more critical in a helpful way.	Study the subject of HELPFUL criticism. How can you do it in a way that will build and not destroy?	Resolute

Stingy	She has a tight grip on our money. That's far better than spending all we have and putting us in the poor house!	Learn how to give generously to yourself.	Supportive
	I will show how to give without wasting money.	Give her things she needs and wants with money you have saved.	Supportive
	She may be fearful of losing what we have. That's a good fear and I will respect that.	Encourage her to enjoy the NOW as she plans for the future.	Kind
She's a jerk!	Though she's a jerk, I will still love her and seek her best.	Write out 20 positive traits for her and share them with her.	Caring

TRIGGERING EVENT	INTERPRE-TATION... FLIPPING	ACTION	FEELING
	I cannot change her but I can change my circumstances.	Spend time with friends.	Anticipation
	I choose not to go berserk over the jerk!	Smile, laugh, dance	Joy
Unfaithful to my father	Somehow she can have sex with another man but still love my father. Thank God she still does.	Focus on her love not on her unfaithfulness.	Peace

	What she is doing is wrong. I don't accept this failure but I do accept her.	Draw up a list of positive traits about your mother. Repeat them to yourself and to her at times. Focus on the good and not the bad.	Serenity
	My father does not like her unfaithfulness but he loves her. I will follow his example.	Love unconditionally.	Love
	I choose to be faithful like my father and embrace his attitudes.	Commit to being faithful in all you do.	Resolution

Does not communicate often	I choose to accept what I can get and not cry about what I cannot.	Praise her when she does talk more deeply	Supportive
	She does communicate but not with words.	I need to be better at spotting her non-verbal cues	Optimistic
	Though she does not talk much, my friends do. At least I have someone to talk with!	Spend time with friends.	Happy
IN-LAWS			
Not loving	They love me but have a hard time showing it.	Write out reasons why your in-laws love you. Smile.	Pleased

	They tend to be selfish, and too bad for them. They are missing out on loving me.	Pump your fist. Say: "I am worth loving."	Confidence
	Though they struggle with showing love, they are great in-laws.	List all the reasons you in-laws are great.	Satisfied
Abusive	This is wrong what they are doing, but I will not let it control how I feel.	Talk with a counselor or a pastor	Resolute
	I hate their abusiveness but I love them.	List their good qualities. Don't let their abuse hide what is good about them.	Peace

	I love them too much to let them continue on this path.	Lovingly confront. Use the sandwich method: Praise/ Confront/ Praise.	Tenacious
Controlling, domineering	I choose not to fight this characteristic but to love and accept them.	Show love to them often.	Loving
	They are afraid of losing control.	Learn ways to help them face their fears. Read. Talk with a counselor about this.	Empathetic
TRIGGERING EVENT	**INTERPRE-TATION... FLIPPING**	**ACTION**	**FEELING**

	I hate it when they try to control me, but I choose not to give into hate but to love them completely.	List ways you can show love.	Honesty
	I resist their control because I like to be in control. I am a lot like them, no wonder we collide.	Accept your role in the tug-a-war for control. Breathe. It's OK. You are normal.	Peace
Absent	My absent in-laws do not mean that I am worthless.	Draw up a list of reasons why you are a good person.	Confident
	I can be happy even if they are gone.	List reasons why you can be happy.	Joyful

	Their continual absence is not good for them or me. Yet I believe that many good things come from what seems not good.	List some good things that could come from their absence. What are some things you can learn from it?	Hope
Alcohol, drug addiction	They are a very sick.	Encourage them to get help.	Empathy
	No matter how many times they fail, I will love them. After all, they are family!	Constantly surround them with your love.	Supportive
	I love them too much to let them continue on in their destructive path.	Do an interventio n.	Resolute

	This behavior is not against me, but is against themselves.	Go to Al-Anon to find help.	Understand
	I cannot change them. They must change themselves.	Quit manipulating and keep encouraging.	Peace
Rage, hit me	I don't deserve this. It's their fault.	Call 911. They must be held accountable	Resolute
	I love them but hate their physical abuse.	I will get them the help they need to get to the bottom of WHY they are so abusive.	Peace

Don't tell me they love me.	They told me they loved me before. That means they still do. I should take their word for it.	Keep saying to them: "I love you," even if they don't respond.	Determined
	The key is not telling me but showing me that they love me. Words are cheap.	Look for ways that SHOW you that they love you. Complement them for this.	Supportive
	Some people are not always the best at communication.	Accept this.	Serenity
TRIGGERING EVENT	**INTERPRE-TATION... FLIPPING**	**ACTION**	**FEELING**

Never or rarely praise me.	I do not need their praise to know what good I do or what positive traits I have.	I will develop a list of positive traits I have and praise myself!	Confidence
	Though they don't praise me, I have friends and family that do!	Thank your friends and family for praising you. Tell them how good it makes you feel.	Gratitude
	They may not like me but I do!	Clap	Joy Confidence
Angry/Temper	I deserved it.	Ask them to forgive you.	Hopeful
	I didn't deserve it. They're an angry, emotional people.	Tell them that their anger hurts you like a bullet to the heart.	Determined

	I do not accept their anger but I accept them. They have many fine qualities that overshadow their anger.	Praise them for their great qualities.	Loving
	Their rage is destroying our relationship but will not destroy me.	See a counselor, your pastor.	Resolute
Critical statements about me	They are so critical of me because they are critical of themselves.	I will help them to be more accepting of themselves by praising them. If I model this they might do that for me.	Hope
	I hate to be criticized but I love them!	Go hug them. Smile.	Happy

	I need to learn how to be more critical in a helpful way.	Study the subject of HELPFUL criticism. How can you do it in a way that will build and not destroy?	Resolute
Stingy	They have a tight grip on their money. That's far better than spending all they have and putting themselves in the poor house!	Learn how to give generously to yourself.	Supportive
	I will show how how to give without wasting money.	Give them things they need and want with money you have saved.	Supportive

TRIGGERING EVENT	INTERPRE-TATION… FLIPPING	ACTION	FEELING
	They may be fearful of losing what they have. That's a good fear and I will respect that.	Encourage them to enjoy the NOW as they plan for the future.	Kind
They are jerks!	Though they are jerks, I will still love them and seek their best.	Write out 20 positive traits for them and share it with them.	Caring
	Just because I have in-laws that are jerks does not mean I'm one.	Counter their jerkiness with love.	Brave
TRIGGERING EVENT	**INTERPRE-TATION… FLIPPING**	**ACTION**	**FEELING**
	I cannot change them but I can change my circumstances.	Spend time with friends.	Anticipation

	I choose not to go berserk over the jerks!	Smile, laugh, dance	Joy
Unfaithful to each other	Somehow they can have sex with another person but still love each other. Thank God they still do.	Focus on their love not on their unfaithfulness.	Peace
	What they are doing is wrong. I don't accept this failure but I do accept them.	Draw up a list of positive traits about your in-laws. Repeat them to yourself and to them at times. Focus on the good and not the bad.	Serenity

Do not communicate often	I choose to accept what I can get and not cry about what I cannot.	Praise them when they do talk more deeply	Supportive
	They do communicate but not with words.	I need to be better at spotting their non-verbal cues	Optimistic
	Though they do not talk much, my friends do. At least I have someone to talk with!	Spend time with friends.	Happy
BROTHER, SISTER			
Not loving	They love me but have a hard time showing it.	Write out reasons why they love you. Smile.	Pleased

	They tend to be selfish and too bad for them.. They are missing out on loving me.	Pump your fist. Say: "I am worth loving."	Confidence
	Though they struggle with showing love, they are a great brother or sister..	List all the reasons your brother or sister is great.	Satisfied
Abusive	This is wrong what they are doing, but I will not let it control how I feel.	Talk with a counselor or a pastor	Resolute
	I hate their abusiveness but I love them.	List their good qualities. Don't let their abuse hide what is good about them.	Peace

TRIGGERING EVENT	INTERPRETATION... FLIPPING	ACTION	FEELING
	I love them too much to let them continue on this path.	Lovingly confront. Use the sandwich method: Praise/ Confront/ Praise.	Tenacious
TRIGGERING EVENT	**INTERPRE -TATION... FLIPPING**	**ACTION**	**FEELING**
Controlling, domineering	I choose not to fight this characterist ic but to love and accept them.	Show love to them often.	Loving
	They are afraid of losing control.	Learn ways to help them face their fears. Read. Talk with a counselor about this.	Empathetic

	I hate it when they try to control me, but I choose not to give into hate but to love them completely.	List ways you can show love.	Honesty
	I resist their control because I like to be in control. I am a lot like them. No wonder we collide.	Accept your role in the tug-a-war for control. Breathe. It's OK. You are normal.	Peace
Absent	My absent brother or sister does not mean that I am worthless.	Draw up a list of reasons why you are a good person.	Confident
	I can be happy even if they are gone and don't visit.	List reasons why you can be happy.	Joyful

	Their continual absence is not good for them or me. Yet I believe that many good things come from what seems not good.	List some good things that could come from their absence. What are some things you can learn from it?	Hope
Alcohol, drug addiction	They are a very sick.	Encourage them to get help.	Empathy
	No matter how many times they fail, I will love them. After all, they are family!	Constantly surround them with your love.	Supportive
	I love them too much to let them continue on in their destructive path.	Do an intervention.	Resolute

	This behavior is not against me, but is against themselves.	Go to Al-Anon to find help.	Understand
	I cannot change them. They must change themselves.	Quit manipulating and keep encouraging.	Peace
Rage, hit me	I don't deserve this. It's their fault.	Call 911. They must be held accountable	Resolute
	I love them but hate their physical abuse.	I will get them the help they need to get to the bottom of WHY they are so abusive.	Peace

Don't tell me they love me.	They told me they love me before. That means they still do. I should take their word for it.	Keep saying to them: "I love you," even if they don't respond.	Determined
TRIGGERING EVENT	**INTERPRE -TATION… FLIPPING**	**ACTION**	**FEELING**
	The key is not telling me but showing me that they love me. Words are cheap.	Look for ways that SHOW you that they love you. Complement them for this.	Supportive
	Some people are not always the best at communication.	Accept this.	Serenity

Never or rarely praise me.	I do not need their praise to know what good I do or what positive traits I have.	I will develop a list of positive traits I have and praise myself!	Confidence
	Though they don't praise me, I have friends and family that do!	Thank your friends and family for praising you. Tell them how good it makes you feel.	Gratitude
	They may not like me but I do!	Clap	Joy/Confidence
Angry/Temper	I deserved it.	Ask them to forgive you.	Hopeful
	I didn't deserve it. They're angry, emotional people.	Tell them that their anger hurts you like a bullet to the heart.	Determined

	I do not accept their anger but I accept them. They have many fine qualities that overshadow their anger.	Praise them for their great qualities.	Loving
	Their rage is destroying our relationship but will not destroy me.	See a counselor, your pastor.	Resolute
Critical statements about me	They are so critical of me because they are critical of themselves.	I will help them to be more accepting of themselves by praising them. If I model this they might do that for me.	Hope
	I hate to be criticized but I love them!	Go hug them. Smile.	Happy

TRIGGERING EVENT	INTERPRE-TATION... FLIPPING	ACTION	FEELING
	I need to learn how to be more critical in a helpful way.	Study the subject of HELPFUL criticism. How can you do it in a way that will build and not destroy?	Resolute
Stingy	They have a tight grip on their money. That's far better than spending all they have and putting themselves in the poor house!	Learn how to give generously to yourself.	Supportive
	I will show how how to give without wasting money.	Give them things they need and want with money you have saved.	Supportive

	They may be fearful of losing what they have. That's a good fear and I will respect that.	Encourage them to enjoy the NOW as they plan for the future.	Kind
They are jerks!	Though they are jerks, I will still love them and seek their best.	Write out 20 positive traits for them and share it with them.	Caring
	Just because I have a brother or sister that are jerks does not mean I'm one.	Counter their jerkiness with love.	Brave
	I cannot change them but I can change my circumstances.	Spend time with friends.	Anticipation

	I choose not to go berserk over the jerks!	Smile, laugh, dance	Joy
Do not communicate often	I choose to accept what I can get and not cry about what I cannot.	Praise them when they do talk more deeply	Supportive
	They do communicate but not with words.	I need to be better at spotting his non-verbal cues	Optimistic
	Though they do not talk much, my friends do. At least I have someone to talk with!	Spend time with friends.	Happy
RELATIVES			
Not loving	They love me but have a hard time showing it.	Write out reasons why they love you. Smile.	Pleased

	They tend to be selfish and too bad for them. They are missing out on loving me.	Pump your fist. Say: "I am worth loving."	Confidence
	Though they struggle with showing love, they are great relatives.	List all the reasons your relatives are great.	Satisfied
Abusive	This is wrong what they are doing, but I will not let it control how I feel.	Talk with a counselor or a pastor	Resolute
	I hate their abusiveness but I love them.	List their good qualities. Don't let their abuse hide what is good about them.	Peace

TRIGGERING EVENT	INTERPRE-TATION... FLIPPING	ACTION	FEELING
	I love them too much to let them continue on this path.	Lovingly confront. Use the sandwich method: Praise/ Confront/ Praise.	Tenacious
Controlling, domineering	I choose not to fight this characteristic but to love and accept them.	Show love to them often.	Loving
	They are afraid of losing control.	Learn ways to help them face their fears. Read. Talk with a counselor about this.	Empathetic

	I hate it when they try to control me, but I choose not to give into hate but to love them completely.	List ways you can show love.	Honesty
	I resist their control because I like to be in control. I am a lot like them, no wonder we collide.	Accept your role in the tug-a-war for control. Breathe. It's OK. You are normal.	Peace
Absent	My absent relatives do not mean that I am worthless.	Draw up a list of reasons why you are a good person.	Confident
	I can be happy even if they are gone.	List reasons why you can be happy.	Joyful

	Their continual absence is not good for them or me. Yet I believe that many good things come from what seems not good.	List some good things that could come from their absence. What are some things you can learn from it?	Hope
Alcohol, drug addiction	They are a very sick.	Encourage them to get help.	Empathy
	No matter how many times they fail, I will love them. After all, they are family!	Constantly surround them with your love.	Supportive
	I love them too much to let them continue on in their destructive path.	Do an interventio n.	Resolute

	This behavior is not against me, but is against themselves.	Go to Al-Anon to find help.	Understand
	I cannot change them. They must change themselves.	Quit manipulating and keep encouraging.	Peace
Rage, hit me	I don't deserve this. It's their fault.	Call 911. They must be held accountable	Resolute
	I love them but hate their physical abuse.	I will get them the help they need to get to the bottom of WHY they are so abusive.	Peace

Don't tell me they love me.	They told be they love me before. That means they still do. I should take their word for it.	Keep saying to them: "I love you," even if they don't respond.	Determined
TRIGGERING EVENT	**INTERPRE -TATION... FLIPPING**	**ACTION**	**FEELING**
	The key is not telling me but showing me that they love me. Words are cheap.	Look for ways that SHOW you that they love you. Compleme nt them for this.	Supportive
	Some people are not always the best at communica tion.	Accept this.	Serenity

Never or rarely praise me.	I do not need their praise to know what good I do or what positive traits I have.	I will develop a list of positive traits I have and praise myself!	Confidence
	Though they don't praise me, I have friends and family that do!	Thank your friends and family for praising you. Tell them how good it makes you feel.	Gratitude
	They may not like me but I do!	Clap	Joy Confidence
Angry/Temper	I deserved it.	Ask them to forgive you.	Hopeful
	I didn't deserve it. They're angry, emotional people.	Tell them that their anger hurts you like a bullet to the heart.	Determined

	I do not accept their anger but I accept them. They have many fine qualities that overshadow their anger.	Praise them for their great qualities.	Loving
	Their rage is destroying our relationship but will not destroy me.	See a counselor, your pastor.	Resolute
Critical statements about me	They are so critical of me because they are critical of themselves.	I will help them to be more accepting of themselves by praising them. If I model this they might do that for me.	Hope
	I hate to be criticized but I love them!	Go hug them. Smile.	Happy

	I need to learn how to be more critical in a helpful way.	Study the subject of HELPFUL criticism. How can you do it in a way that will build and not destroy?	Resolute
Stingy	They have a tight grip on their money. That's far better than spending all they have and putting themselves in the poor house!	Learn how to give generously to yourself.	Supportive
	I will show how how to give without wasting money.	Give them things they need and want with money you have saved.	Supportive

TRIGGERING EVENT	INTERPRE-TATION... FLIPPING	ACTION	FEELING
	They may be fearful of losing what they have. That's a good fear and I will respect that.	Encourage them to enjoy the NOW as they plans for the future.	Kind
They are jerks!	Though they are jerks, I will still love them and seek their best.	Write out 20 positive traits for them and share it with them.	Caring
	Just because I have in-laws that are jerks does not mean I'm one.	Counter their jerkiness with love.	Brave
	I cannot change them but I can change my circumstances.	Spend time with friends.	Anticipation

	I choose not to go berserk over the jerks!	Smile, laugh, dance	Joy
Unfaithful to each other	Somehow they can have sex with another person but still love each other. Thank God they still do.	Focus on their love not on their unfaithfulness.	Peace
	What they are doing is wrong. I don't accept this failure but I do accept them.	Draw up a list of positive traits about your in-laws. Repeat them to yourself and to them at times. Focus on the good and not the bad.	Serenity

Do not communicate often	I choose to accept what I can get and not cry about what I cannot.	Praise them when they does talk more deeply	Supportive
	They do communicate but not with words.	I need to be better at spotting his non-verbal cues	Optimistic
	Though they do not talk much, my friends do. At least I have someone to talk with!	Spend time with friends.	Happy
GRAND CHILDREN			
Fighting	This is not unusual. After all, they are children!	I will help them to learn to be givers and not takers and thus reduce much of the fighting.	Peace

TRIGGERING EVENT	INTERPRE-TATION... FLIPPING	ACTION	FEELING
	One of my grandchildren needs special attention. That's the reason they are picking on the other child.	Give special attention to them. Help them to FEEL accepted.	Resolute
	The grandchildren want MY attention. I have neglected them and thus they are telling me that through their fighting.	Set aside special time for THEM. Go to the park, take them out for a special treat, play a game with them.	Loving

	I have been too lenient when they fight. I need to have consequences.	Set up a penalty and reward system. Have them help you do this. When they fight they get penalized. When they have a day of peace they get rewarded.	Confidence
Sick	Young children need to see the doctor 4 or 5 times a year. So this is normal.	Relax. Smile. Your grandchildren are normal.	Acceptance
	Though getting up in the middle of the night is a pain, my grandchildren are worth it all.	Quite complaining and embrace the happiness of raising grandchildren.	Joy

	They need immediate, emergency attention and will rush them to the hospital where they can hopefully get help.	Take deep breaths. Pray. Thank God that he is with you and will help.	Brave
Failure in school	Failing in school doe not mean they are a failure.	Quite fixing the blame and fix the problem.	Resolute
	They may be trying to get attention.	Spend more time with them, listening, helping, Understand.	Gentle
	The problem could be a number of things: The school, the teacher, other grandchildren, myself, or my child.	Get some counseling. Look at the possibilities and move intelligently toward a solution.	Smart

	I need to get my grandchild tested to make sure I am not pushing him too hard.	Work with principle or trained therapist. Find results.	Care
	They are failing because of problems in our home.	Get help. Fix the problems. Fix yourself!	Bold
Disobedient	It is partly my responsibility to help them learn how to obey.	Help grandchildren to know WHY they need to obey.	Optimistic
	The rebellious behavior is normal, but must come to an end.	Draw up a list of PAINFUL results for rebellious behavior. May sure they understand that intentional rebellion will be painful for them.	Resolute

TRIGGERING EVENT	INTERPRETATION... FLIPPING	ACTION	FEELING
	Disobedience is a mark of immaturity. And does it surprise me that they disobey since they are but children?	ACCEPT they are children. Smile. ACCEPT too your responsibility to help them to grow up.	Acceptance
	This gives me a chance to help them to learn how to be a better person.	Use disobedient behavior as a teaching tool. In one since their disobedience becomes a POSITIVE time for you to help them to grow into the person they should become.	Encouraged

Lie	They are fearful of being caught. And that's good!	Set up positive/ negative reward system for lying. Make it worthwhile for them to tell the truth.	Optimistic
	They don't understand why lying is wrong and hurtful not just to others but to themselves.	Explain to them the consequences of lying. Relax. If you do, lovingly, they will learn.	Relaxed
Mean, bully	They are trying to feel important.	Draw up a list of positive traits about them. Help them to embrace these.	Loving

	They fight and bully because they don't see the rewards that come from being nice.	Help them to see the difference from being a GIVER and a TAKER. Givers are the ultimate winners in life.	Understand
	He's/she's mean but I still love them!	Smile. Keep loving. Hug them.	Peace
Boyfriend, girlfriend problems	This is normal.	Draw up some directions TOGETHER.	Cooperative
	Their hormones are working. That's good.	Help them understand what's happening and how to be successful with the opposite sex.	Empathy

	Sexual involvement is natural but not good until married.	Talk openly about sexual involvement discussing options. Lead them in a commitment to wait.	Hopeful
	Living together.	Love. Be firm with your convictions. Accept WHO they are not WHAT they are doing (if this is in line with your moral convictions)	Friendly
Granddaughter gets pregnant	They made a wrong choice but we can now make some good choices for her and the baby.	Smile. Help her look at the options.	Compassion

	This is not the end of the world. In a few years the mistake will be forgotten and we will be joyful in this new gift of life!	Forgive. Don't fix the blame but fix the problem. Work together to do it.	Confident
Drinking before age 21	This is not good, but not the worst thing that can happen. Most children experiment at this age.	Relax. Breathe. Guide. Have a good, open talk. Accept who they are, not what they did.	Peace
TRIGGERING EVENT	**INTERPRE -TATION... FLIPPING**	**ACTION**	**FEELING**

	Though this is normal at this age it is a wake up call to step in and help.	Show love and concern. Ask: Where did thy get the drinks, who where they with, describe how did it feel? Make this a learning situation.	Acceptance
Drug involvement	Thank God I discovered their involvement!	Don't panic. Breathe. Develop a plan to help.	Resolution
	Their drug involvement is not good. My discovery is.	Pray. Get counsel from your pastor or counselor. Read. Plan. Be positive. Your attitude will be a great help.	Positive

	Though they are hooked, I can get help.	Find a place to take them for help. Don't condemn. Love. It may take tough love to pull them through.	Compassion
Rebellion	This opens my eyes to the fact that I must take stronger action. And I will!	Lead. Show tough love. Draw up a list of things that must change. Be courageous. Praise, then discipline, then praise.	Passion

	I need to make sure that I am not creating this resistance by the way I act and lead.	Have an open conversation with your child. Find out what they really want. Help them develop a plan to get it.	Sincere
Shy, withdrawn	This is not necessarily a bad thing.	Accept that they have a quiet personality	Peace
	They may be struggling with inferiority.	Help them to see their strengths and to move ahead in these areas Praise them.	Satisfied
Grumpy	It could be that they always seem tired and this grumpiness is the result.	Sit down with them and develop a schedule. Let them take leadership.	Tender

TRIGGERING EVENT	INTERPRE-TATION... FLIPPING	ACTION	FEELING
	I need to become more aware about sleeping habits, eating, and be aware that they might be on drugs.	This is a time for you to wake up and pay attention. You are the grandpare nt. Be one. Be involved.	Hopeful
Lazy	I need to find what motivates them.	Draw up with them a reward system that would motivate them.	Joy
	Part of it is my problem. I was too involved in their lives and let this habit get rooted.	Be aware. Do not be afraid to confront, lovingly. Be confident.	Hope

DIVORCE			
Fighting over child custody	I need to quite fighting and do what is best for the children.	Sit down with someone who is not emotionally involved and have them help you think this through.	Determined
	My husband/ wife wants to win. I want what is right for both of us.	Refuse to battle. Smile. Relax. The judge will see your giving attitude.	Peace
	Just because my former mate did me wrong, I don't have to use the children to get even with them.	Listen to your former mate. Fix the problem without fixing the blame. Work TOGETHER instead of against each other.	Resolute

	My value and worth is not tied to this custody battle.	Draw up a list of positive traits about yourself. Recite them to yourself.	Confidence
Seeing the other woman/man	Though they left me, I have the strength to carry on.	List your strengths. Smile.	Thankful
	Though I am tempted to feel jealous, I instead choose to want the best for my former husband/wife.	Pray a prayer of blessing for them. Breathe deeply.	Peace
	I choose not to hate but to love.	Be gracious to them. Smile. Praise her/him.	Courageous

Holiday/ visitation problems	There are problems to work out but I will do my best to do what is right without resentfulness.	Stop blaming and calm down. Breathe. Smile. The world is not coming to an end because all does not work as planned.	Content
	They are late again, but at least I get to see the children.	Focus on the good and not the bad.	Cheerful
	They are too busy again to see the children. That's their loss and my gain because I get to be with them more.	Focus not on what they are NOT doing but what YOU can do.	Optimistic
Child support late…again	It's late, but it will get here.	Don't be a perfectionist.	Content

	I choose not to battle him/her but to let the legal system take care of this.	Call your lawyer. Set a court date.	Relaxed
	They are doing this to wound me. But I refuse to let it make me feel bad.	Don't get caught up in revenge thinking. Breathe. Smile. If you do what is right you will be the winner in the long run.	Liberated
TRIGGERING EVENT	**INTERPRE-TATION... FLIPPING**	**ACTION**	**FEELING**
	He/she's a jerk. That doesn't surprise me. And they will be that the rest of their lives.	Accept who they are. Don't try to change them. Be positive about what you can do.	Certainty

Judge ruled against me	One ruling does not mean it's set in concrete. The ruling can change.	Work with your attorney.	Hope
	I was trying to wound my former mate by asking for too much.	Change. Get out of the blame trap. Focus on seeking to heal your wounds and not on wounding your former mate.	Forgiveness
Running out of money for attorney	There are other ways to get help, organizations who could give me advice.	Check with the county to get help. Call your pastor. Friends may have some ideas.	Brave

| | I have been trying to win and have not moved toward resolution. No wonder it has cost me so much! | Get out of the cycle of resentment and revenge. Breathe. Forgive. Seek counseling to help. | Encouraged |
| Child says they hate you | I'm glad she shared this so I can deal with it. | Own up to the fact that you may have made some mistakes. Have a heart to heart talk with your child and ask them to forgive you. | Resolute |

	I can understand why they are so angry with me. This divorced has ripped at their security. They feel abandoned.	Don't give like for like. Show lots of concrete love. And be patient. Time heals.	Patience
	I did make some mistakes and own up to it. So this hatred is not without reason.	Ask for forgiveness.	Tranquil
TRIGGERING EVENT	**INTERPRE-TATION... FLIPPING**	**ACTION**	**FEELING**
DEATH			
HUSBAND, WIFE, CHILD, PARENT, OTHERS			

	I'm shocked! And shouldn't I be?	Embrace your grief. Cry. Let your emotions out.	Release
	I will miss them but I will always cherish them.	Express gratitude.	Grateful
	Changes are sad but not always bad.	List the good that will come from this death.	Thankful
Funeral	Yes, they died and I will miss them very much, but I refuse to focus on my loss but rather on my gain for having them in my life.	Draw up a list of all the great memories you have. Smile.	Joy

	I grieve, and that's good. Grieving is healthy.	Read a book or article on grief and the various stages you will go through.	Reassured
Loneliness overcomes you	I sure miss them! But I will make it and lean on the friends and relatives that love me.	Don't sit and stew. Go out with a friend even if you don't feel like it.	Resolute
	I do feel loneliness and that's OK. I accept it as part of losing the one I love.	Cry. Release your feelings. Then smile. Say: "I'm going to make it!"	Acceptance

	I am alone, but not really. God is always with me. His loving presence is there for me to tap into anytime I need it.	Pray. Talk with God. And let him talk with you. Journal your responses.	Peace
Trust, Probate issues	There are a lot of things I have to do, but I will make it as I take one day at a time.	Draw up a list of things to do and set dates when you will do them. Breathe. Take your time. You will make it through.	Confidence

TRIGGERING EVENT	INTERPRE -TATION... FLIPPING	ACTION	FEELING
FRIENDS			
Had a fight	They sure were testy today. But that's OK. I accept them for how they are.	Draw up a list of reasons you are friends. Think of the history, all that you have done together.	Appreciation

	Wow! I was sure in a foul mood today and helped fuel the flames of our argument. Instead of blaming myself and feeling bad, I'm going to admit to my friend my poor responses.	Call your friend and ask for forgiveness. State what you did and that you take full responsibility for what happened.	Peace
	In a few days things will be better. Time always heals if we let it.	Smile. Relax. Wait. Let time pass before you deal with the situation.	Patience
Unkind remarks or actions	These do not reflect who I am as a person. I will not take ownership of them.	Quit repeating the words and actions. Stop your desire for revenge.	Resolute

| I did a wrong thing and deserved their remarks and actions. | Smile. Accept the remarks and go one step further. Thank the person for their actions even though it could have been done in another, more peaceful way. Talk with them about a better way to let you know of your mistakes. | Acceptance |

	Their anger and actions show me that I need a new friend.	Don't hang around people who abuse you. Patience is good, but opening yourself to abusive speech and action is not.	Resolution
Jealous or envious remarks or actions	They want what I have which means that I do have it pretty good. For that I am thankful.	Instead of focusing on their jealousy, focus on the good things and the personal gifts you have.	Thankful

	Instead of getting angry at their jealousy or envy, I will seek to understand and to help them find freedom from these feelings and actions.	Study jealousy and envy and how you can help your friend rise above it.	Empathy
	They want to possess me and thus take away my freedom to be who I really am.	Have an honest talk. Tell them you want to be their friend but they can't be possessive.	Liberation

No true friends	It is true that I do not have a close friend, but that doesn't mean I will never have one.	Relax. Breathe. Tell yourself that you will one day have a close friend if you continue to be a giver instead of a taker.	Peace
TRIGGERING EVENT	**INTERPRE -TATION... FLIPPING**	**ACTION**	**FEELING**
	I do have a close friend - God.	Pray. Spend time with this friend.	Joy
	I have many acquaintances. One of them may become a close friend one day.	Keep engaged with people. Go to places where people are - church, social and service clubs.	Resolute

	I need to quit focusing on FINDING a close friend and instead BE a close friend to someone else.	Go out to lunch, serve others. Quite looking and move on to becoming.	Hope
Friend moved	They moved but we can still keep in touch and continue our relationship.	Text. Email. Phone. Facebook. Skype. There are all kinds of ways to keep in touch.	Confidence
Lost a friend	Though I lost a friend, I can and will find another.	Be a friend and you will find another. List those whom you can begin to nourish.	Acceptance

	Come to think of it, they were never a true friend anyway.	Thank God that you can get on with your life and move into a friendship that will be satisfying.	Hope
NEIGHBORS			
Loud music, pool parties	Instead of being frustrated I will gently let them know that they need to turn down the music.	Talk. Be nice. Be polite. Smile. Ask for a favor.	Peace
	I'm feeling angry which is a signal that I need to do more than I have done.	Call the police. Anger is an emotion that can drive you to do what is right. Keep calm in your anger. Breathe.	Calm

Don't mow grass, messy yard.	It's their yard. They can do with it what they want. I will quit being so perfectionist.	Breathe. Smile. Relax. It's not a big deal. There are more important things to get disturbed about.	Tranquility
TRIGGERING EVENT	**INTERPRE-TATION... FLIPPING**	**ACTION**	**FEELING**
Kids are bullies	I cannot control their kids but I can control mine. I will do what I can do without worrying about what they should do.	Keep you children from the bullies. Build a fence. Talk with them about what they can do.	Resolution

I can't control them but the county or city can.	Call the authorities and discuss what can be done. Let any anger move you to a peaceful solution. After talking with the parents you could also get other parents in the neighborhood to band together and work on a solution.	Peace

	I choose not to hate these kids but feel compassion for them. Bullies are insecure and unhappy.	Think through ways to engage these kids in something that would help them to find themselves. It may be a project, or an invitation to a youth program at church, or some other social activity like scouting. PRAY for wisdom.	Empathy
Rude behavior, public cursing,	I acknowledge that my neighbors are jerks. But I choose not to be a jerk in my response.	Be loving, kind, generous, helpful.	Resolute

	Underneath the tuff exterior there is someone who is needy.	Pray about how you can meet those needs. Instead of pushing them away, invite them over for dinner, or a pool party, or to church.	Empathy
	I choose to LOVE my enemies and not hate them.	Pray: "God, how can I show love to them in a real, tangible way?"	Hope
Refuse to repair a broken fence.	Broken fences are not nearly as bad as broken relationships. I choose to work on our relationship.	Don't push away your neighbor. Talk. Be friendly. Do not make the fence a BIG issue. Find a way into his heart.	Caring

Got home T.Ped (toilet papered)	What a mess! This is the price for being the focus of attention.	Focus on the good of being T.Ped and not the bad. Smile when you clean it up. Laugh.	Release
TRIGGERING EVENT	**INTERPRE-TATION... FLIPPING**	**ACTION**	**FEELING**
Barking dog	Not again! I choose not to focus on the bark and turn on some music.	Turn up the music.	Peace
	Instead of stewing, I'm going to talk with my neighbors and find a solution to their barking dog.	Don't go with anger. Accept. Praise dog. Work on a solution together.	Confidence

SCHOOL PROBLEMS			
Teacher acts like he/she doesn't like me	So what. I'm going to study, do well, and get through the year. Next year I will have another teacher.	Quit fixing the blame. Be the best student you can. Fighting the teacher will only bring damage on yourself.	Determined
	I messed up and gave her a bad time. No wonder he/she doesn't like me. But I will settle down, do my school work and make him/her proud of me.	Accept that you screwed up. Take steps to correct that. Affirm the teacher - praise him/her. They will love it.	Courageous

TRIGGERING EVENT	INTERPRE-TATION… FLIPPING	ACTION	FEELING
Students aren't friendly	Some students aren't friendly but not all of them. I choose to be friends with those who accept me.	Don't fret about some rejection. Be thankful for those students who do accept you.	Accepting
Failed a test	OK, I failed. But that doesn't mean I'm a failure. I will do my best next time to get a passing grade. Who knows, if I study hard enough I might get an A!	Don't sit and stew. There is another day. With hard work you will do better.	Confidence

SOCIAL GROUPS Country clubs, Service clubs, Travel clubs			
Domineering leadership	Why am I always fighting in myself when someone gets their way and I don't get mine? Let it go. Is it really that bad?	Release your desire to compete. Breathe. Relax. It's not worth the fight.	Tranquility
	Domineering people are often insecure. I will help this person to feel more secure and at peace within themselves.	Instead of pushing this person away, draw them closer. Become an expert on them. Go out to lunch, a ball game.	Resolute

| | With patience I and others can replace this leadership. Patience is better than war! | Wait. Relax. Your time and the time for other leaders will arrive. | Patience |
| Nasty member | That was a nasty remark. But I choose not to focus on that and rather think about things that are good and wholesome. | Practice Philippians 4:8. Think about these things. | Peace |

TRIGGERING EVENT	INTERPRE-TATION... FLIPPING	ACTION	FEELING
	Nasty people are too often unhappy people. I will seek to help this person to find the true source of happiness.	Encourage them to read my series on depression , or anger. Better yet, buy them a copy. You can tell them that this book really helped you and have been giving away copies to your friends.	Resolute
Jealous or envious remarks or actions	They want what I have which means that I do have it pretty good. For that I am thankful.	Instead of focusing on their jealousy, focus on the good things and the personal gifts you have.	Thankful

	Instead of getting angry at their jealousy or envy, I will seek to understand and to help them find freedom from these feelings and actions.	Study jealousy and envy and how you can help your friend rise above it.	Empathy
	They want to possess me and thus take away my freedom to be who I really am.	Have an honest talk. Tell them you want to be their friend but they can't be possessive.	Liberation
Chapter 3 WORK PROBLEMS			

TRIGGERING EVENT	INTERPRE-TATION... FLIPPING	ACTION	FEELING
PEOPLE AT WORK			
Angry, cantankerous, mean, judgmental, unkind	They can act this way, but I don't have to respond in like manner.	Do not let their negative approach infect your workday. Smile. Breathe. Relax.	Relaxed
	This makes me mad. But I will use my anger to bring about change.	Think through ways to combat their anger. Others at work may help you.	Resolute
	Though their behavior is unacceptable, it won't spoil my day.	Smile. Don't let others control how you feel. Report to boss if necessary.	Peace

	This outburst only shows me that they need help	Pray about what do to help this person feel more adequate and loved.	Empathy
Vulgar	This angers me. I will do something so it doesn't happen again. Then I and others will feel better.	Talk with management. Are they breaking HR rules? Do the loving thing: get this person help.	Healthy anger
	I choose to be tone deaf and not let this person disturb me.	Breathe. Relax. Smile. Come up with a list of positive characteristics about this person. Share them.	Calm

Irresponsible on a project.	This is frustrating. Yet I will channel my frustration into fuel to get this project done.	Lay out a plan to complete the work without the total commitment of irresponsible person.	Resolution
	This is a good opportunity to share my frustration with my irresponsible co-worker, but do it with love.	Don't just accuse. State the problem. Praise them for some other good work. Then share your frustration. Listen.	Anticipation
Dishonesty	They lied to me to protect themselves. It's good to protect yourself. I need to help them learn how to protect themselves without lying.	Think about how your co-worker can speak the truth in ways that will still protect themselves.	Satisfied

TRIGGERING EVENT	INTERPRE-TATION... FLIPPING	ACTION	FEELING
	Often people that lie do it habitually. They are so fearful of being rejected that they are always covering up even when they don't need to.	If the person is open, role play situations and how the person can answer truthfully without losing face.	Kind
Flirtatious	This is wrong behavior that angers me. I will use this anger to motivate me to bring about change.	There are laws against this kind of behavior. Warn the person and then report if they continue.	Resolute

	This person thinks that sex is the goal of life. I feel sorry for them.	Pray for them. Ask God to help you minister to them and open their eyes to their real needs that they are masking.	Bold
Discrimination	This is wrong! My anger will move me to do something.	Report the discrimination. Then relax. You did the right thing.	Peace
	They are from an older generation and don't fully grasp what they are doing. I can forgive them for this.	You can forgive, but you must confront too in love. They need to adjust to new situations and laws.	Courageous
BOSS, MANAGEMENT			

Demanding	He's more old school and dictatorial. But his heart is good and he wants the best for the company and me.	Focus on his good qualities rather than what irritates you.	Peace
	He's ambitious and I'm not. That's why he is the boss and I'm under his leadership.	Accept his role and be thankful for yours.	Acceptance
	My irritation is my problem not his.	Quit blaming and learn how to put yourself under the authority of leadership. Relax. Breathe. Say that it's OK.	Resloution

Unfair	Life often is not fair, but I can still be happy.	Practice Philippians 4:8 in your thinking.	Release
	Yes they are unfair, but I still have a job that pays the bills.	Be thankful for your job. Quit focusing on the negative parts of it.	Joy
Gave you a poor review	Though I don't like things pointed out that I need to change, I do want to improve. So I am thankful for this review, the incentive it gives me to be better.	Be grateful. Thank you boss for helping you to be a better employee.	Grateful
TRIGGERING EVENT	**INTERPRE -TATION... FLIPPING**	**ACTION**	**FEELING**

	Reviews can be painful. But as they say: "No pain, no gain."	Set up a plan to achieve all the things you might be lacking so that the next review will be better.	Resloution
Flirted with me	This makes me mad. And that's good. It will move me to report this behavior.	See HR or an attorney if inappropria te behavior is happening. Document it.	Confident
	Though their behavior is wrong, I encourage d it and need to stop doing that.	Recognize your involvemen t and stop it.	Determined

Refused to give me a raise	Though I don't like the outcome, I'm proud of myself for having the courage to ask.	Pat yourself on the back. Smile.	Happy
	Their reasons for not giving me a raise were good. I accept that.	Breathe. Relax. Smile.	Understand
	This company is stingy. But as least I have a job!	List reasons to be thankful.	Grateful
He/she got angry at me	I felt attacked unfairly. Yet, they didn't fire me! I still have a job!	Focus on the good things you have rather than the things you don't have.	Thankful

	I hate it when people get angry with me, but this time I deserved it. I really screwed up.	Admit this to your boss. Affirm that you will do better. Be thankful that they were honest with you.	Courageous
	Their temper is out of control. This kind of abusive behavior must stop. This last incident motivates me to do something about it.	Report to HR, move to another department or find another job.	Resolution
WORK			
Boring	I admit it's boring, but at least I have a job!	Focus on the good things your work helps you achieve.	Thankful

TRIGGERING EVENT	INTERPRE-TATION... FLIPPING	ACTION	FEELING
	This job is boring because I have lost interest in it. If the truth were told, I am responsible for the boredom.	Choose to make the job interesting, or to at least see the interesting parts of your work.	Resolute
	I am thankful for a boring job. It gives me time to pray and to use my mind in other ways that are good and beneficial.	If you are on an assembly line you could use your time to pray for others as you do mundane tasks. You can also think about God and worship him, and get paid for it!	Joy

Long hours	I'm tired but at least I get paid for it.	Relax. List the reasons your job is good.	Grateful
	What is long? Our ancestors worked 10, 12, 14 hours a day six days a week. Why am I sweating 9-10 hours a day, five days a week? I'm overreacting.	Relax. Smile. Long hours are not necessarily harmful. God said that work is important. Be thankful. Enjoy your job. Do all things to glorify God.	Joy
	Yes, I have to work long hours, but at least I have some time for my wife/ husband and family.	Use the time you have off to focus on your wife, husband and family. Don't hibernate.	Purpose

Fired	Wow! I didn't see that coming. Though upset, I will move on and find a better job.	Be thankful for the job you had. Be thankful for the job you will find. Relax. Say to yourself: "Things will get better."	Confidence
	I screwed up. I choose to take my mistakes and learn from them.	Evaluate what you did wrong. Accept it. Don't fret. Learn from your mistakes. The future is going to be bright!	Optimism

| | I was wrongly fired, but I will not focus on these wrongs but move ahead to a better future. I see my firing as a step for a better future. And that's great! | Be thankful you were fired. This painful experience is what you need to open up a better future for you. Smile. | Hopeful |
| Must move to another city | Ouch! This is not going to be easy. But I will make the transition and help my family to do the same. | Breathe. Write out the positive good that can come from a move. | Hopeful |

	This is not going to be easy. Yet it's great to be promoted and to get a sizable salary increase.	Clap your hands! Good things are coming.	Joy
Asked to lie	Instead of fretting about this, I will come up with a plan where we can tell the truth, and still accomplish what the boss wants.	Come up with that plan and talk with the boss. Do not condemn, but seek to guide them into a more truthful way.	Resolution
	If I refuse to lie I may lose my job, and is that so bad? God may be leading me to something better.	Refuse to lie. Be kind about it. Come up with an alternative. Be bold.	Confident

Denied a raise	Though I don't like the outcome, I'm proud of myself for having the courage to ask.	Pat yourself on the back. Smile.	Happy
	Their reasons for not giving me a raise were good. I accept that.	Breathe. Relax. Smile.	Understand
TRIGGERING EVENT	**INTERPRE-TATION... FLIPPING**	**ACTION**	**FEELING**
	This company is stingy. But as least I have a job!	List reasons to be thankful.	Grateful

Stuck	Because of my education and experience I'm stuck in this job. Rather than fight it, I choose to accept my place in the workplace and be thankful for what I have.	Acceptance Thankful Stop using the word, "stuck," and instead use words like, "I am lucky to have a job at all," or "I may be stuck at work, but I get to come home to the love of my life."	Hope
Stuck			Hope

TRIGGERING EVENT	INTERPRE -TATION... FLIPPING	ACTION	FEELING
CAN'T SLEEP	I choose to focus on the sleep I do get rather than fuss over the sleep I don't get.	Be thankful.	Relaxed

My lack of sleep is the result of anxiety. I can't expect to sleep if I continue to worry.	Stop the anxiety and worry. How? Count your blessings. See if you can get to 500. Read books on worry and anxiety and practice their advice. Remember : T + A = F. Change your thoughts and you will sleep better.	Resolution
I'm getting older and my bones hurt. I will accept my age, the problems that come with it.	Accept. Breathe. Thank God that you are getting older. It beats the other option!	Peace

	This lack of sleep motivates me to talk with my doctor. He may have a medication I can take.	There are sleep helps and aids as well as relaxation techniques you could benefit from. Look these up online.	Determined
Got on the scale and see I have gained a lot of weight!	Agh! Instead of standing here and blaming myself, I will get involved in a good program to lose weight.	Call Weight Watchers or follow some other program. Be patient. It took months to get to where you are. It will take months to get trim again.	Confident
	I'm too heavy but God still loves me, and so does my husband/ wife.	Smile. Say: "God loves me no matter what I look like."	Joyful

	Fat is beautiful!	Quit focusing on your looks and enjoy your life and the people you love.	Satisfied
	I love who I am, but I know that my weight may pose health problems. So, my love for myself means that I will take are of myself and do what the doctor says.	Eat anything you want - just cut it in half. This way your taste buds will be satisfied and you will lose the weight that is needed.	Purposeful

Don't like my face, breasts, hips, hair, nose	I choose to accept how God made me. He said that I was "fearfully and wonderfully made."	Say: "Thank you God for the way you made me. I accept it and choose to be proud of my body and treat it with pride." Buy nice clothes, style your hair, get profession al advice on how to look the best.	Confidence
TRIGGERING EVENT	**INTERPRE -TATION... FLIPPING**	**ACTION**	**FEELING**
	I'm going to change some areas with plastic surgery. Why not get what will make me look better?	Smile. Good changes are going to happen	Anticipation

	I'm not Miss America, but I am me. And I love me for who I am.	Smile. Quite comparing yourself with others. You are the best you in the world!	Pleased
Surgery needed	The bad news is that I need surgery. The good news is that they can fix my problem.	Be thankful. Smile. Laugh. Say: "It's going to be alright."	Confidence
	I'm scared. But I'm in good hands. So I choose to set aside my fear and focus on the positive outcome.	Thank God that he will be with you. Thank him for the healing he will bring.	Thankful

	Instead of asking why this is happening to me, I will ask: why not? God must think that I am capable of handling it, and that this test will make me a stronger person.	Relax. Breathe. Don't fight it. Accept the operation and thank God for what he will teach you.	Comfortable.
	Surgery sucks. But the results are great!	Focus on the outcome - healing and full health.	Glad
More hair is falling out!	I accept myself and the way I look.	Look in the mirror. Smile. Say: "I love who I am."	Confident

	I'm shocked about this loss. But that's not the end of my life. There are things I can do to still look normal.	See a doctor. Go online and check out options for either growing new hair or other alternatives. Be thankful. There are options.	Serene
	Since God loves me the way I am, I choose to love myself this way, even if I am losing my hair.	Write out a note an put it on the mirror: "You are BEAUTIFUL/ HANDSOME!" Signed GOD.	Encouraged
Bad breath, body order	Whew! That's bad. But I know what to do and will take care of it.	Gargle, use deodorant, perfume or cologne.	Relieved

	I smell bad and can't seem to fix the problem. I will see a doctor.	Call a doctor. Smile. You are going to get it fixed.	Pleased
	Smelling bad does not mean I am bad.	List all your good qualities. Praise yourself.	Cheerful

Chapter 5
HEALTH PROBLEMS

TRIGGERING EVENT	INTERPRE-TATION... FLIPPING	ACTION	FEELING

Cancer	I'm in shock! When I learn more I will relax and do what I need to do.	Feel the grief. It's OK. Then determine to get the facts about your cancer. Though cancer is a fearful word, many cancers can be treated.	Hope
	I AM not cancer. It does not define who I am. I only have it and someday I hope not to have it.	Too many say " I am," instead of "I have." For example people say: "I AM depressed." No! They only have depression. Depression does not define who they are. So say "I have…"	Realism

I choose not to let fear reign but instead believe that I am strong enough to face this setback.	Say: "I am strong. I can face it with God's help. I need not be afraid."	Comfort
Nothing can ultimately kill me because of God's life in me, I will live forever! Sorry cancer, I win. You lose.	Say: "I am not afraid to die. Why? God promises me eternal life. And that eternal life is far better than what I'm experiencing now."	Joy
I am hopeful that my cancer will be cured. This hope will always be alive and make me joyful.	Say: "I have hope." Smile. Laugh. Embrace your healing.	Joy

| Nothing can kill me. Cancer can't, nothing can. No matter what happens, I will live forever! | Clap your hands. Say: "I win, cancer loses." Smile. God's eternal life is in you and that can't be taken away. Never! | Confidence |
| This cancer is a gift, not a curse. God loved me enough to allow me to have this disease. | Personalize Romans 8:38-39. "Nothing can separate me from the love of God. Cancer can't, all the pain and sickness can't, NOTHING!" | Overjoyed |

Lost my breasts to cancer	This is sad, but not tragic. Why? My breasts are not who I am. I did not lose ME and never will.	Thank God that you had breasts. Thank him again that you life was saved through their loss. Praise God that you are a soul and not a thing like breasts.	Grateful
	Bye bye breasts. Hello life!	Quite focusing on the loss and instead focus on what you have gained - life!	Blessed

	My femininity is not tied to my breasts but to my brain. And I still have my brain which thinks feminine thoughts.	Say: Beauty is not just on the outside but also on the inside. I am a beautiful woman.	Confidence
TRIGGERING EVENT	**INTERPRE -TATION… FLIPPING**	**ACTION**	**FEELING**
Headache	Headaches are not forever.	Breathe slowly and deeply. Relax your shoulders. Smile.	Hope
	My headache is telling me that something is wrong. I'm going to see my doctor.	Make an appointme nt. Try some acupressur e points (see google). Some are used to relieve headaches .	Reassured

Heart attack	Thank God I'm still here!	Take an aspirin, call the ambulance. Breathe.	Optimistic
	This is going to be a long journey back. But I will make it!	Smile. Say to yourself: "I'm going to make it."	Satisfied
	Though I will not beat myself up, I really deserved this heart attack. The way I ate, drank, smoked and worked set me up for this.	I choose to become a more responsibl e person. I deserve it, my wife/ husband, family deserve it, my friends deserve it.	Resolute
	I am not afraid to die, but I still choose life in the here and now.	Smile. Embrace life.	Confidence

Other medical problems like: ALS, Multiple sclerosis, Parkinson's, Palsy, Diabetes	This is serious. And I'm serious in my desire to beat this disease or to at least hold it at bay.	Clap your hands. Pump your fist (a victory pump). Say: I will not let this disease destroy me."	Determined
	Though this is bad, real bad, I choose to focus on what is good in my life and the lives of others.	Write out a list of all the blessings you have. Try to get to 500. Then smile. Life is good!	Grateful

| | Though I feel some grief and sadness about what I have, I will not let this grief and sadness overwhelm me. I have a great mate, children, friends and church. I choose to focus on all I have and not what I don't have. | Smile. | Cheerful |
| Knee, ankle, hip pain | Pain tells me something is wrong. I will find out what it is. Pursuing this will help me feel better. | Call the doctor. Look on the internet. Ask friends who may struggle with the same type of pain. | Hopeful |

TRIGGERING EVENT	INTERPRETATION... FLIPPING	ACTION	FEELING
	Everyone of these can be replaced. I can be a bionic man or woman!	Check with your orthopedic surgeon. Find out when you should move ahead with these operations.	Content
	Yes, these hurt, but my head doesn't! The drugs I take for pain are the best option for now.	Don't focus on the pain. Focus on pleasure you can have, now - chocolate candy, a glass of wine, a bowl of cherries.	Satisfied

	I can't do anything right now about the pain, but I can accept it and not complain about it. This I choose to do.	Accept. Embrace the pain. God is allowing it to touch you for your good. Let the pain produce that goodness. It will!	Meaning Purpose
Sexual problems (pain, erection, feeling, lack of desire)	My problem is not the end of the road but only a beginning to discovery of what is wrong so that I can make it right.	Relax. Say: "Things are going to get better." Contact a doctor, check the internet, talk with trusted friends.	Resolution
	This problem is not unusual. I can get help.	Smile. Don't blame yourself. Keep being proactive.	Peace

Life is more than sexual pleasure. I choose to focus on other pleasures for now.	Make a list of all the pleasures you are experienci ng like: Pleasure of food, music, nature, art, warmth by a fire, friends, church, a cool breeze, talking with God, etc.	Pleasure
I choose to thank God for the sexual pleasure I have had rather than cry about what I don't have.	Praise God. Be thankful. Laugh. Life has been good.	Happiness

Dementia, alzheimer's, or other brain problems	Loss of memory is so devastating. Yet I choose to focus on the years I or another had good memories. There were many joy-filled times. Wow!	Let yourself grieve. That's good. It's good grief. But don't get stuck in it. To get out, focus on the many years of good memories. List at least 500 of them. Recount them to friends and family.	Joy
	Rather than crying over spilled milk, I will thank God that I had some milk to spill!	Thank God for the memories.	Grateful
TRIGGERING EVENT	**INTERPRE-TATION... FLIPPING**	**ACTION**	**FEELING**

Though this person does not seem to be there, they are still God's child, and I choose to treat them with love and kindness.	Be loving. Be kind. God is there in them. You are taking care of God! What a privilege!	Amazement
They do not know me, but I KNOW THEM, and love them.	Thank God that at least one of you has memories that can be recalled… YOU! So not all memories are lost. Share these memories with that loved one at times and smile. God is good.	Appreciation

Operation on heart, lungs, other organs	This is serious, but I am hopeful that all can be repaired.	Smile. You are in good hands, doctors and God.	Hopeful
	I'm in good hands, the doctor's and God's. What is there to fear!	Let God hold you in his arms. Relax.	Peace
Other dreaded health crisis like, septic shock, Ebola, hepatitis C, meningitis, malaria, pneumonia, etc.	I'm very sick. I could die. Yet I'm still alive! As long as I can breathe I will ask God to help me. He will not abandon me.	Smile. Relax. Say: "God is with me. I need not fear."	Secure
	Thank God I have help!	Trust your doctors. They are there to get you through.	Confidence

	Though I feel some grief and sadness about what I have, I will not let this grief and sadness overwhelm me. I have a great mate, children, friends and church. I choose to focus on all I have and not what I don't have.	Smile.	Cheerful

Chapter 6 MONEY PROBLEMS			
TRIGGERING EVENT	INTERPRE-TATION… FLIPPING	ACTION	FEELING
Can't pay bills	No money does not mean no hope. There are people and places where I can find help.	Call your pastor. Call a friend. Don't go it alone. Don't beg. Just show your need and find counsel to help you get over the crisis.	Resolute

	I may be worth less, but I'm not worthless. My value is not tied up in money or things but rather in who I am.	Focus on WHO you are and not WHAT you have or don't have.	Confidence
	I'm going to quit fixing the blame (on others or myself) and fix the problem.	I will look at both short term and long term solutions.	Determined
Disagreement over money	We disagree, but if we listen to each other actively, we will come to an agreement.	Listen. Seek to understand more than to be understood.	Resolute
	I am going to stop trying to be in control and find a solution that works for both of us.	Breathe. You don't always have to win.	Peace

	I choose to quit loving money and the things I can buy and choose instead to love my wife, husband, children, others. They are what is valuable.	Realize that money can never buy happiness. Let its control of you go. Release it. Give as much of it away as you can. And you will find peace and joy.	Peace and Joy
	I need God in my heart instead of money in my wallet.	List the riches that come from spending time with God.	True Happiness
Investment problems	We just lost 50% of our investments. Though that hurts, we have our lives and each other.	Be patient. The markets go up and down. Don't panic. All will be well.	Peace

I need to quit being a gambler and learn better how to get a good return with sufficient security. This loss is a motivation to do that.	Invest in what is broad based (10,000 + stocks). Invest also in a broad based bond fund. Then sit back and relax. You will do great!	Security
I will save 10% and invest it WISELY. I will also give 10% to my church and other charitable organizations.	Draw up your plans. Follow them without fail. You will always have sufficient money, plus the great feeling of helping others.	Joy

Poor credit	Whether this is my fault or someone else's, I choose to fix the problem and not fix the blame.	Read Dave Ramsey at <u>daveramsey.com</u>. He will show you how to get out of debt and begin to learn how to save and spend your money.	Resolute
TRIGGERING EVENT	**INTERPRE-TATION... FLIPPING**	**ACTION**	**FEELING**
	I admit it. My credit is poor. There is no reason to deny it. This is what is.	Accept the facts: your credit is poor. Accept that if you don't do anything, it will stay poor. Take action. There is good advice on the internet.	Resolute

| Loss through gambling | I got caught up and took more risk than I should have. It's all my fault and I take the blame. | Stop gambling. You may have an addiction. Get counseling. Find out why you think money will make you happy, or why the thrill of risk moves you. | Determined |
| | My husband/ wife needs help. Instead of blaming them, I will encourage them to get this addiction under control. | Check out gamblers anonymou s. It may be the help you need. And relax. Help is on the way. | Content |

	It hurts a lot more to lose than the joy of winning. Gambling is no longer fun. I'm going to find some other way to enjoy life.	Ask: Why am I gambling? If you enjoy it and can stand the loses, OK. But if it is a desire to get rich quick, and it hurts you financially when you lose, stop.	Inquisitive
Mortgage not accepted	I wanted that house but either we need better credit or more down payment. If I'm patient, I can improve both.	Relax. This is not the end of the road. Work or a better credit score and save more money.	Resolute

	I don't have to have that house to be happy.	Review again what true happiness is: not having the right things but being the right person.	Joyful
	That was a nice house. But we will find another one that will better fit our budget.	Smile. Say: "We will find another house. Patience always wins!"	Determined
Car breaks down, furnace worn out, refrigerator goes caput, need new roof, etc.	I accept that things wear out. Yet we don't have the money to fix them, at least yet. I will find a way to finance this need.	Don't throw up your hands and give up. There is ALWAYS a way to find a solution. Relax. Pray. Get outside counseling.	Resolute

| There goes our savings! But thank God we have a savings! | You saved for a rainy day and now you will reap the benefit. That $50, $100 a month put aside in an emergency account really adds up over a period of a few years. Relax. You're OK. | Gladness |
| Instead of asking: "WHY is this happening to me?" I will ask: "WHAT am I going to do? WHY questions lead me to dead end answers. WHAT answers move me into action. | What? Brainstorm. You will be given an answer. Then smile. Everything is going to be OK. | Confident |

TRIGGERING EVENT	INTERPRE-TATION... FLIPPING	ACTION	FEELING
Christmas spending and no extra	I don't have much money to buy gifts, but I have a brain that can help me be creative so that I can still give.	Think: What can you make that would satisfy as a gift? You could make candy, cookies, make a craft, or give a gift of a dinner: one that you would fix. Be creative. There are a lot of ways to give without breaking the bank.	Creative

| I cannot give things this Christmas, but I can give myself: some time to wash their windows, to clean their house, to wash their car, to take care of their kids. | Figure a way you can be a giver. This could move your Christmas giving to a whole new level! | Inspired |

	Christmas is after all about Jesus. I can always give him my heart and love others as he loved.	Draw up a love list. List ways you can love them. It doesn't have to cost a dime. Idea: You could write love letters to all your relatives and friends. Tell of your love. Show your love. And it will be the best Christmas ever!	Joy
Always worrying about money	I am going to "seek first the kingdom of God and all these other things will be given to me."	Relax in God's love and generosity.	Peace

I choose not to worry but to instead pray to God and be specific with my requests. Then I will thank him for taking care of us.	Thankful prayer is the secret to overcoming worry. Don't look at what you don't have, but at the blessings you do have.	Security and peace
Worry NEVER works. I will stop worrying and focus instead on all I have. Focusing on what I don't have makes me sad. Seeing what I do have gives me joy.	Draw up a blessings list. Write down at least 500. List material, physical, social, relational blessings. There are thousands!	Focused

I just inherited a bunch of money and don't know what to do	Of course I don't know what to do. I have never been in this place before. But I will take my time and find out what is best.	Be patient. Find a good financial counselor. Don't rush into anything.	Resolute
	I have questions, but will not allow these questions to torpedo my joy. This money is meant to be a blessing and not a worry.	Clap your hands. Shout joyfully. Thank God for the blessing of this inheritance and the wisdom for what to do.	Happy

	I can now finally give generously to my church, to a charity, to others in need.	Get help from your pastor or trusted friend. Giving is one of the most joyous things you can do.	Joy filled

**Chapter 7
CHURCH,
GOD,
RELIGIOUS
PROBLEMS**

TRIGGERING EVENT	INTERPRE-TATION... FLIPPING	ACTION	FEELING
			Joy filled
CHURCH			

My pastor just left	Instead of crying over his leaving, I will thank God for his ministry in my life.	Focus on the good that he did rather than on the empty space he will leave.	Peace
	I will miss him but God will provide another good pastor	Pray: "Thank you God for a good pastor. Send us another one who can lead us closer to you."	Thankful
	Grieving a loss is good. But I won't get stuck there. I will move on to praise God for his provision of a new pastor.	Grieve. Then release the old pastor and be open to welcoming a new one.	Anticipation

Another boring sermon	He is not a great preacher, but he sure is a great pastor. And I like that!	Focus on his good qualities and not the bad.	Serenity
	OK. His preaching stinks. But that can be fixed. There are courses that teach pastors how to give inspiring sermons. I will gently encourage him to take one of these.	Don't sit and complain. DO SOMETHING! He needs help, and you know what to do. There are secrets to giving a good sermon. Help him discover them.	Determined

	His messages are not good, but I know where to find food for my soul. He is not the only source.	Read your bible. Read good religious materials. Find a pastor whose sermons inspire. Listen. Smile. You have all you need.	Optimistic
I hate the music	I don't like it but others do. And that's good that some are being ministered to.	Accept that others have different tastes in music.	Peace

	Instead of fighting about the music, I'm going to suggest we have two services, one traditional and the other contemporary.	Move toward a solution rather than fixing the blame. There is a way if your are patient.	Patience
The pastor's wife is not friendly, or dresses inappropriately, or is not involved.	OK. There may be some things about her I don't like, but there are many other things in the church I like. I choose to focus on these.	Quit looking at what may be a problem and rejoice instead on what is good.	Joy

		ACTION	FEELING
	We didn't hire the pastor's wife, we hired him. And he is doing a great job.	Quit focusing on things you cannot change but rather on things that are worthy of praise (See Philippians 4:8).	Grateful
TRIGGERING EVENT	**INTERPRE-TATION... FLIPPING**	**ACTION**	**FEELING**
Changed a belief or moral practice	This is wrong and I will work to make it right.	Know why the new belief is not in accord with historical teaching and why the practice is only a capitulation to a changing society.	Determined

	It this continues I will change churches.	Talk with the pastor. Tell him of your disappointment. Be loving but firm.	Resolute
	Though I don't like the changes, I will stay in this church to be a light and a conscience of what is right and good.	Be loving. But do not be afraid of affirming what is true and right.	Bold
Too many cliques	Cliques are only groups of people who like to be around each other. I need to form my own clique.	Quit blaming and do something about it. Work at becoming friends with others. Pray. God will lead you.	Confidence

Always asking for money	Why shouldn't they? They need it.	Quit blaming and start giving.	Compliance
	They are focusing on the money rather than talking about ministry. I will help them to learn how to show what God is doing so that people will open up their purse strings. This will bring joy to their giving.	Help your pastor or leaders to see WHY people give and what is the greatest motivation. People love to give to a cause that changes lives.	Hope
Too much gossip	I can't control others, but I can control myself. I refuse to gossip.	Make a pledge. Refuse to pass on juicy information about another parishioner.	Determined

	I choose to speak up when I think someone is gossiping, without coming across as judgement al.	Be courageou s. Stop the stream of gossip. You can say: "I think that should be kept private. Can we talk about something else?"	Courage
TRIGGERING EVENT	**INTERPRE -TATION... FLIPPING**	**ACTION**	**FEELING**
Pastor caught in adultery or some other sin	Ouch! What a disappoint ment! He needs our prayers.	"God forgive him. God restore him. God, use this to develop him to be a more devoted person to you.?	Caring

	Our pastor is human and has sinned. I feel compassion toward him and want to see him get healed.	Quite fixing the blame and fix the problem. Why did he fail? Get him help. He needs love and not condemnation.	Compassion
The vote went against what I wanted	I choose to submit my will to the church and to the will of the people. My way is not always the best way. In time I will see a good outcome.	Accept the vote. Don't speak against it unless it is immoral or not in line with church teaching. Affirm those who voted differently.	Acceptance
GOD PROBLEMS			
I question God's love	Instead of doubting God's love, I am going to embrace it.	Thank God for his love.	Thankful

I can't understand why so many bad things are happening to me. And that's my problem, I'm trying to understand the infinite God with my finite mind.	Thank God that you don't understand him. If you did, he would only be a human person. But he is beyond us, to wonderful for us to imagine. Praise him.	Joy
How can I question God's love when he gave his all for me? God proved his love by sending his Son to die. What love!	Clap your hands to the LORD. Praise him. Smile. Someone loves you very much - God!	Jubilant!

| | To doubt only brings depression. And I sure don't want that! I chose to believe and to trust even if I don't fully understand. After all, that's what faith is, isn't it? | Believe. Trust. Receive God's love. | Good |
| God seems to be so distant. I feel alienated. | If God is so distant, who moved? I must have. I can do something about that, and I will. | Pray prayers that are honest. Pour out you heart to God. Then thank him that he is with you even if you don't feel it. Smile. Clap your hands to God. FAITH it and you'll FEEL it. | Hope |

TRIGGERING EVENT	INTERPRE -TATION... FLIPPING	ACTION	FEELING
	My doubts are pushing God away. I choose to get back to trusting instead of doubting.	Say: "I'm going to trust in the LORD with all my heart. This means that I will not be leaning on my own understand ing." Proverbs 3:5 personaliz ed.	Peace
How can God be all powerful and loving and allow all this evil in the world…in MY world?	Yes, God is all powerful and loving and allows all this evil in the world because he didn't START IT. We did. And he is willing to give us the power to STOP IT.	Think about ways to stop the evil in your neighborho od, in your family, in your life. Then do it with God's power.	Resolute

	I am going to quit fixing the blame and instead fix the problem.	Evil is here because people don't know how to really live. Live is "evil" spelled backwards. So many things are backwards today. I will do what I can to reverse that.	Confidence
I don't know God	I'm not going to wallow in my ignorance but determine to get to know God personally.	Read the Gospel of John. Where it says believe, do it.	Experiential knowledge

	I may not know God but he knows me. And that's a good thing.	Thank God that he knows you in and out. He says about you that: "You are fearully and wonderfully made."	Joy
RELIGIOUS PROBLEMS			
I'm tired of all these religions claiming to be true. Can't they all get along?	All religions can't all be true, but they can all have some truth. I need to find out which one is true and follow it.	Read: *If There Is A God, Whose God Is God,* by Dr. Paul J. Young. This will give a lot of insight.	Resolution

Rules, rules, rules. I'm sick of rules!	Christianity is a belief system. Christianity is also a behavioral system. There are rules to follow and obey. More than anything Christianity is a RELATIONSHIP. I choose to be in that relationship with Jesus.	When you put the relationship first, keeping the rules come easier. You keep them not because you have to but because you want to. Focus on developing this relationship through prayer, Scriptural reading, church.	Acceptance
I'm tired of religion. I want to do what I want.	Religion does take effort. But when God lives in me and I allow him to work, the effort becomes easier.	Jesus said: "Come, take his yoke, and we will find REST for our souls." What you need to do is TRUST and not just TRY.	Peace

TRIGGERING EVENT	INTERPRE-TATION... FLIPPING	ACTION	FEELING
	I've done that before and got into a big mess. Life without God is like walking down a dark alley. Anything can happen. And it won't be good!	You want to be free. Look at a train. It has to run on tracks. What if it wanted to go on its own, leave the limitation of the tracks and set its own course? Wreckage. That happens to us to without religious rules (the 10 Laws). They are really steps to freedom.	determined

I'm afraid I won't get to heaven	I can't by myself. I can through Christ who is the way, truth and the life.	John 3:16 says: He who believes on the Son (Jesus) will have eternal life. That's heaven!	Joy
	I choose not to live in fear but in accepting the love of Christ for me. He is more interested in my going to heaven than I could ever be. And that makes me feel really good!	Relax. Smile. Say: Because of Jesus, I can go to heaven. All I need to do is keep following him.	Security

Chapter 8 PERSONAL OR MORAL FAILURE			
TRIGGERING EVENT	**INTERPRE -TATION... FLIPPING**	**ACTION**	**FEELING**
MORAL FAILURE			
I committed adultery	I admit my failure. I confess my sin. And I am determined to never let this failure happen again.	Confess to mate and to God. Accept forgiveness. Understand why you did what you did and how to avoid this kind of moral colapse again.	Sorrowful joy

I let a busy, empty life get me into this mess. If I fill my soul with God, I will never do this again.	Meet with God each day through prayer and Scripture meditation. St. Augustine said: "Our hearts are restless until they find their rest in thee, O Lord."	Joy
I will feel a lot better if I become a giver and not a taker.	Give your life away - to your mate, your children, to others. Jesus said: "it is more blessed to give than to receive."	Happiness

| | Though I screwed up big-time, God still loves me. | "Nothing can ever separate us from God's love." St. Paul

Smile. Shout Thankful to God for his love and forgivenes s. | Celebration |
| I was dishonest | At least I recognize it. I will seek from now on to tell the truth. It feels a lot better! | Write down the reasons why honesty is the best policy. Embrace your reasons. | Determined |

I lie because I'm afraid of others. I need to analyze why this fear is running my life. If and when I get free of it, I will never need to lie again.	Think through why you are fearful. Learn how to "speak the truth in love." Think of ways you can speak the truth without offending another person. Speaking the truth does not mean you are blunt. Be soft, be caring, be courageous. Speak the truth.	Courageous

Anger, rage, temper	I feel such power when I'm in a rage. It feels good. But the results of it are disastrous. I hurt the people I love, and that doesn't feel good. I am going to get help so that I will not wound those I love anymore.	Get help now before it's too late. Learn about what triggers your anger. Buy my book: Dr. Paul's TOTAL RELIEF, Anger. It will give you insight and a deep down answer to what is going on in your soul.	Resolute
	I need to learn how to get angry without sinning - harming others. And I will do that.	Read Ephesians 4:23-32. Learning to be gentle and to forgive is foundational to ridding yourself of the harmful type of anger.	Determined

TRIGGERING EVENT	INTERPRE-TATION... FLIPPING	ACTION	FEELING
	Why is it that I don't feel anger? Anger is a healthy emotion that will move me to make positive changes in myself and others. I choose to embrace this kind of healthy anger.	Injustice should make us angry. And that anger will be the fire that starts the engine of change. BE ANGRY… but do not sin.	Intention

Drug, alcohol addiction	Instead of fixing the blame, I will fix the problem starting now.	Admit your problem Change your behavior one day at a time, one minute at a time. Join AA Fill your soul with the one who loves you and created you - God.	Hope
	Though my addiction makes me feel great in the short term, it is destroying me and my life will be wasted. I choose to no longer live for short term satisfaction but long term joy and happiness.	Don't just say no to your addiction but say yes to family, to others, to God, to that joy filled life that is to come. Saying "YES" is more powerful and life changing.	Positive

Gluttony	Boy do I love to eat! But what's driving that. Is there something eating at me? I choose to find out.	DISCOVER what is your underling problem. Seek counseling. Look into your soul. Too often we seek to fill our empty souls with food when only God can satisfy.	Curious
	Food has become like a drug. I'm addicted. Now I know what to do. Get help with my addiction.	Get help. Join a food addiction group that's much like AA. Listen to others, their failures and successes. It will help you to break your addiction. Smile. You are going to get better.	Freedom

PERSONAL FAILURE			
Bankruptcy	Instead of fixing the blame I will fix the problem. I can always blame myself and others, but I choose to rebuild my credit and get back on a good financial footing again.	ADMIT why you got into trouble. DETERMINE to not make the same mistakes again. READ Dave Ramsey at daveramsey.com to get great financial insight. SAY: "Tomorrow will be better." Smile. Relax.	Confidence

Can't keep a job	I want to blame everyone else but myself. Anger and resentment have been ruling my life. And that may be my problem. I have a chip on my shoulder and need to correct that. If I do, I may become a better employee.	Take the blame. Fix the problem. Get counseling. Relax. Your next job opportunity may result in a long term job. Smile. It will happen!	Happiness
	I choose from now on to seek to please my employer rather than myself. If I do this I will find favor and keep my job.	List ways you can please a boss. Then do it.	Determined

Can't make friends	I need to quit looking for friends and BE a friend to someone.	Write out a list of people whom you would like to be friends with. Go out for a cup of coffee. Church is one of the best places to make a friend, or some other social or service club like Lions, Kiwanis, Rotary, etc. SMILE. You are going to make a friend!	Hope

Chapter 9 SUDDEN DISASTERS, EMERGENCIES LOSS			
TRIGGERING EVENT	**INTERPRE-TATION... FLIPPING**	**ACTION**	**FEELING**
Earthquake, tornado, hurricane, flood	This is frightening. But I need to focus on getting safe instead of being overcome with fear.	Get into a safe room or outside. Let your fear move you to safety.	Determined
	The destruction is terrible! Yet I'm still alive! My family is safe. And that brings me joy!	Focus on what you have and not what you don't have.	Joy

All I lost was stuff. And stuff can be replaced. If I can stay focused all will be well in a year.	It is OK to grieve the loss of stuff, but put it in perspective. Focus instead on what you have - your lives and the ability to replace the stuff.	Peace

At this time I can only quote Holy Scripture: *"There is no test that happens to us that not common to humankind. But God is FAITHFUL to provide with this test a way to escape the emotional blasts of it so that we might be able to endure and find peace and joy again."* I choose to believe and rest in this promise.	Read this promise in I Corinthians 10:13. Read also James 1:2-4 about why we should be joyful in trials. List the reasons. Embrace the reasons. Smile. Yes, everything looks bad. Remember that pancakes are made of bad stuff, but when heated, they're great!	Grief surrounded by JOY!

CAR breaks down, FURNACE worn out, REFRIGERATOR goes caput, APPLIANCES, TV, STOVE, ROOF, LAWNMOWER need replaced, etc.	I accept that things wear out. Yet we don't have the money to fix them, at least yet. I will find a way to finance this need.	Don't throw up your hands and give up. There is ALWAYS a way to find a solution. Relax. Pray. Get outside counseling.	Resolute
	There goes our savings! But thank God we have a savings!	You saved for a rainy day and now you will reap the benefit. That $50, $100 a month put aside in an emergency account really adds up over a period of a few years. Relax. You're OK.	Gladness

TRIGGERING EVENT	INTERPRETATION... FLIPPING	ACTION	FEELING
	Instead of asking: "WHY is this happening to me?" I will ask: "WHAT am I going to do? WHY questions lead me to dead end answers. WHAT answers move me into action.	What? Brainstorm. You will be given an answer. Then smile. Everything is going to be OK.	Confident
	This is all going to take time and money, but thank God I have some or will get my hands on enough to get us through.	Be thankful. Don't get focused on the loss but on the solution. There is a way out. Smile.	Joy

Electricity shuts off and it's 10 degrees in the winter or 100 degrees in the summer!	Instead of asking WHY? I'm going to ask WHAT? This will bring me to a solution that will make me feel good.	WHY? questions paralyze. WHAT? questions set us free to find answers. You can always grab a blanket or a fan, or drive to Walmart, take a book and sit in the patio section! Come on - you can come up with something.	Satisfied

Bulb burns out, COMPUTER crashes, loose all your files on the computer, FROZEN PIPES, food in FREEZER THAWS due to lack of electricity, etc.	No matter what happens my joy is not tied to things or events. Emergencies and tragedies happen. But they will not take away my peace and joy.	REFUSE to let events get you down. You are bigger than that. REPEAT: "Nothing can take away my joy." REJOICE. This is not living in denial, but understanding what life is truly about. Life is not things. It's relationships, the greatest being our relationship with God that can never be lost.	Joy

| Weather problems: ICE SNOW BLIZZARD HEAT RAIN WIND COLD HUMIDITY | I choose to relax. There is nothing I can do to stop this weather. So why fight it? Enjoy it. And soon the weather will change. It always does. | Relax. Breathe. Embrace the weather, don't fight it. If you fight it you will lose every time. List reasons why what is happening is good. Dig deep. You can find good in anything. | Peace |

TRIGGERING EVENT	INTERPRETATION... FLIPPING	ACTION	FEELING
Frost or freeze killed everything	Wow! What a cold spell! And what a disaster with my flowers! They were so beautiful and awesome, a beauty that can be replaced. And I will do it after the freeze lifts. My yard will look good again!	Plants are not like people. They can be replaced. Be thankful that this is true. And don't complain. Griping about the weather only brings anxiety. Relax. Let the weather do what it does and YOU DO WHAT YOU CAN. You are in charge.	Confidence

Other emergencies:
TIRE BLOWS
ENGINE STOPS
CARPET STAINED
TOILET OVERFLOWS
CLOTHES RIP
FURNITURE scratched
WINDOW BREAKS
CAR WON'T START
LOSE CAR KEYS
NO MILK
INSECTS ATE PLANTS
WEEDS!
KIDS THROW UP
BUSH DIES
GUTTER won't drain
WATER too expensive
SPRINKLER CAPUT
FOOR CRACKED
SHIRT NOT IRONED
HOUSE A MESS
PET

Instead of focusing on the problem, I choose to focus on the solution. Complaining only gets me upset. I choose to come up with a way to fix the problem.

Know the truth: there is a problem. Know the solution: It can be fixed. DO THE SOLUTION. Don't sit and sulk when you can fix it. Know that getting upset only delays getting to the answer.

ACCEPT that things break or go wrong. Don't be surprised! Come on! That's life. But it's also true that things can be fixed. That's life too. And when you stop

Undiminished JOY!

Chapter 10 PERSONAL FEARS			
TRIGGERING EVENT	**INTERPRE -TATION... FLIPPING**	**ACTION**	**FEELING**
Going through a tunnel	I hate tight places, but the car is moving at 60 miles an hour which means that I will be though in less than a minute. I like that!	Breathe deeply. With 5 deep breaths you will be through the tunnel. Yippee! Smile. You are going to make it.	Calm

I choose not to fight my fears. I won't resist getting uptight. I'm human and humans have fears.	Embrace your fears. Breathe deeply and don't resist. RELAX. Don't be afraid of fear.	Freedom
Instead of focusing on my fear, I choose to replace negative thoughts with grateful thoughts. I am going to thank God that he is with me in the car as we travel through the tunnel. I am surrounded by his love.	Don't fight the fear, replace it with God's presence. Focus on him, his love, his protection. Say: "Thank you God that you are with me now. I drink in your presence and love." SMILE. You are going to be OK!	Peace

Public speaking	I choose to not focus on myself but on the people who need to hear what I have to say. This is not all about me, but about them.	Breathe. Relax. Say: "I'm a little nervous, but that's OK. My focus is not on me anyway but on them. And that makes me feel good.	Optimistic
	I'm scared but I'm also brave. I am willing to face my fears without letting them paralyze me. And that makes me feel good.	Accept the fear. Don't run but embrace it and let it help you to be a better speaker. How? It will make sure you plan and prepare well. This means that you will be ready and will not fail. Breathe. Relax. You are going to do great!	Confidence

Shucks. My fear is a common fear. Most people have it. But most do not have the courage to face the fear and do it anyway. I choose to feel the fear and speak anyway. I am not afraid of fear!	Say: " I'm anxious, but that will not stop me." Smile. Pump your fists. You are winning over fear..	Victory

Interview for a job	Because this interview is critical and I need this job, I feel anxious. And that's OK because this anxiety will keep me sharp and make sure I do and say the right things.	Don't focus on your anxiety but let anxiety do what it's supposed to do - keep you at your very best.	Determined
Going over a bridge	I hate high places, but the car is moving at 60 miles an hour which means that I will be though in less than a minute. I like that!	Breathe deeply. With 5 deep breaths you will be over the bridge. Yippee! Smile. You are going to make it.	Calm

TRIGGERING EVENT	INTERPRE-TATION... FLIPPING	ACTION	FEELING
	I choose not to fight my fears. I won't resist getting uptight. I'm human and humans have fears.	Embrace your fears. Breathe deeply and don't resist. RELAX. Don't be afraid of fear.	Freedom
	Instead of focusing on my fear, I choose to replace negative thoughts with grateful thoughts. I am going to thank God that he is with me in the car as we travel over the bridge. I am surrounded by his love.	Don't fight the fear, replace it with God's presence. Focus on him, his love, his protection. Say: "Thank you God that you are with me now. I drink in your presence and love." SMILE. You are going to be OK!	Peace

Getting on an elevator	I hate enclosed places and heights, but the elevator is moving quickly which means that I will be on the right floor in less than 30 seconds. I like that!	Breathe deeply. With 5 deep breaths you will be through at the right floor. Yippee! Smile. You are going to make it.	Calm
	I choose not to fight my fears. I won't resist getting uptight. I'm human and humans have fears.	Embrace your fears. Breathe deeply and don't resist. RELAX. Don't be afraid of fear.	Freedom

	Instead of focusing on my fear, I choose to replace negative thoughts with grateful thoughts. I am going to thank God that he is with me in the elevator as we travel to the next floor. I am surrounded by his love.	Don't fight the fear, replace it with God's presence. Focus on him, his love, his protection. Say: "Thank you God that you are with me now. I drink in your presence and love." SMILE. You are going to be OK!	Peace
MRI's, Cat scans, tight places	I hate tight places, but this will be over in less than 30 minutes. and that's good. I will enjoy the rest of the day in open spaces. I like that!	Breathe deeply. Smile. You are going to make it.	Calm

I choose not to fight my fears. I won't resist getting uptight. I'm human and humans have fears.	Embrace your fears. Breathe deeply and don't resist. RELAX. Don't be afraid of fear.	Freedom
Instead of focusing on my fear, I choose to replace negative thoughts with grateful thoughts. I am going to thank God that he is with me as I take this test. I am surrounded by his love.	Don't fight the fear, replace it with God's presence. Focus on him, his love, his protection. Say: "Thank you God that you are with me now. I drink in your presence and love." SMILE. You are going to be OK!	Peace

Shy Have to meet people	I'm shy and find it hard to meet new people. Yet I refuse to let my shyness control me. I choose instead to greet them with a smile, look at them in the eye and be gracious. Conquering my shyness makes me feel good.	Smile when you meet people. Relax. You are not giving in to your shyness.	Confidence

| It's OK to be shy. Many people are. But I will not let it keep me from meeting people. | Don't run from your fear. Feel the fear of meeting meeting people, and do it anyway. This way YOU control your fear instead of letting it control you. | Resolute |
| Instead of focusing on my feelings of shyness, I choose to focus on the person I'm meeting. I want to be attentive to them. When I do this, I feel great! | LOOK at the person. What is the shape of their face, the color of their hair and eyes. SAY: "I'm going to focus on them." ASK: "How can I love them? FEEL compassion for them. | Love |

TRIGGERING EVENT	INTERPRE-TATION... FLIPPING	ACTION	FEELING
Flying	I hate flying, but the airplane is moving at 500 miles an hour which means that I will be at my destination soon. I like that!	Breathe deeply. Smile. You are going to make it.	Calm
	I choose not to fight my fears. I won't resist getting uptight. I'm human and humans have fears.	Embrace your fears. Breathe deeply and don't resist. RELAX. Don't be afraid of fear.	Freedom

	Instead of focusing on my fear, I choose to replace negative thoughts with grateful thoughts. I am going to thank God that he is with me in the airplane. I am surrounded by his love.	Don't fight the fear, replace it with God's presence. Focus on him, his love, his protection. Say: "Thank you God that you are with me now. I drink in your presence and love." SMILE. You are going to be OK!	Peace
Chapter 12 **FACING THE FUTURE**	Instead of focusing on my fear, I	Don't fight the fear,	Peace

TRIGGERING EVENT	INTERPRE-TATION... FLIPPING	ACTION	FEELING
Worry about having enough money	I'm going to stop worrying and start planning.	Stop the "what if" game. Start a plan. This will stop the worry	Calm
	Worry does not accomplish anything. I choose to stop it and instead work on a plan for the future.	Breathe. Smile. Go to work on a plan.	Inspired

No matter what happens I will have my life. I will never starve. There will always be an organization, a church or other people to help if all goes wrong.	Look at the telephone book - all the social organizations and churches who would stand with you in time of need. Relax.	Peace
God tells me not to worry. Why? He will always be with me and provide for every need.	Tell God, "Thanks!" Smile. You are in good hands - God's.	Happy

Fear of:	Fear is good. But I refuse to let it control me. I will use fear to avoid problems only and not let it disable me. When I do this I will be at peace.	Do not fear fear. Accept it. Be thankful for what it does. It wants to protect you. And that's good. Choose to use the positive aspect of fear and not its negative effect. Drink in peace.	Calm
DYING WAR CANCER DISEASE DEATH OF PARTNER GOING TO HELL ROBBERY RAPE MURDER HOUSE ON FIRE CAR ACCIDENT			
	No matter what happens to me, God is with me. NOTHING can touch me unless God permits it. He is out for my best.	Thank God! Read I Corinthians 10:13. Breathe. Relax. You're in good hands.	Relaxed

| There are so many things to fear! So many things can go wrong. Buy why worry about them? It destroys my joy in the present. So I choose to focus on good things that can happen or are happening. There are so many. | List all the good that is happening. Rejoice. Life is good! | Joy. |

Dr. Paul

Education:

University of California, Fresno, B.A in English

Dallas Theological Seminary, Th.M (Masters in Theology)

Biola University, Doctorate of Ministry with emphasis on psychology (working with Talbot School of Theology, Rosemead School of Psychology and other schools)

Dr. Paul Joseph Young helped grow one of the largest churches in the Dallas/Ft. Worth area as its pastor, working with thousands of people, developing his skills both as a minister, communicator and a counselor. For seven years he was C.E.O. of Community Bible Study International, working in over 60 countries of the world.

Dr. Paul's communication skills has made him a favorite speaker around the world. He lives with his wife Diane. They have five children and 14 grandchildren.

More than anything, Dr. Paul lives to help people find the joyful life they deserve.

OTHER BOOKS BY DR. PAUL

1. **Lethal Discord** a Catholic Thriller. This has been called a "page turner" by many who read it. You will live the story and learn about your faith as you read this compelling novel.

2. **Lethal Discord companion guide** with questions that will help you dig deeper into the novel.

3. **Great Men of the Bible - Saint Paul, his secret to success.** The story of his success can be yours!

4. **The Personalized Bible, Philippians**
This book will help you to make right choices about feeling great. I take the book of Philippians, a book in the New Testament, and write it as if it were written to YOU. Reading this book for 30 DAYS in a row could have a great impact on the joy you experience every day.

5. **Amazing Women of the Bible** - women you never knew before. Read this dramatic presentation of these great women! You will not be the same.

6. **Know What You Believe** - the catechism for today. A simple way to learn what you believe, a method for you and your family can use that will give you a depth of understanding of your Catholic Faith.

7. **You Can Change Your World** - a powerful book that gives us the secret to changing our world. It's explosive!

8. **How To Finish Well.** A Catholic book for Retired men who want to make the most of their retirement.

9. **Potato Salad for the Depressed Soul** - Magical steps to take to blast away depression while making potato salad! This is a crazy book that could change your life and bring the joy you are looking for.

10. **TOTAL RELIEF SYSTEMS SERIES** (3 books in each category - 9 books total). These are books written to help people overcome their emotional struggles and find peace, purpose, and joy. They take a person into an in depth journey to find restoration and healing for their souls.

   - **Dr. Paul's TOTAL RELIEF -** Depression

   - There are *NINE books in this series*, books that will liberate you from depression and anxiety, setting you on the pathway toward JOY, the kind of life you dreamed of.

11. **Dr. Paul's FEELING GOOD ToolBox.** There are so many things that happen to us with interpretations that guarantee that we feel bad. Want to change your interpretations and actions so you feel a lot better? This is a must read. It will TRAIN you to think and act right.

12. **The NOTE.** Why has the music left your soul? What is life all about? How can I get music back into your inner being, a song that fills me with hope and joy? This book is both a visual and verbal parable about the NOTE and how he can change you life…NOW!

13. **30 Days To Making Your Wife Feel Special.** This book could radically change your marriage…in only 30 days. Take the challenge. You nor your wife will be the same.

14. **If There Is A God, Whose God Is God?** Who's right, the atheists? The agnostics? What about the eastern religions, or the Jews, or Islam? And then all those Protestants…why do Catholics believe that the Church is really Catholic? Lots of questions. Lots of answers. It will be a faith-building adventure.

15. **The Unexpected Visitor.** What would happen if you opened your front door and saw Jesus standing there, wanting to come in a stay for a few days. What would you do? How would you act? Would you make any changes? This book delves into a couple who had to allow Jesus to stay with them and the changes it made in their lives.

16. **How To Be An IMPACT MAN** - a powerful book that will help men to become spiritual forces in their homes, Churches, workplaces and the world.

   *This book is also published in a young adult edition designed for college student and young single men.

17. **The IMPACT MAN *Daily Walk*** - a daily devotional for men that will take them to another level in their walk with God. It's practical and powerful! (also in a Young Adult edition).

18. **How To Be An IMPACT WOMAN** - a powerful book that will help women to become spiritual forces in their homes, Churches, workplaces and the world.

19. **The IMPACT WOMAN *Daily Walk*.** This daily read includes all the books of the bible from Genesis to Revelation with each day focusing on I.M.P.A.C.T. Reading it every day will revolutionize your life.

20. **GUARANTEED RECOVERY from a loss.** Have you lost something dear, a relative, friend, home, job, reputation or money? This book is for you. I teach a simple T.A.P. technique for overcoming loss and finding peace and joy again.

21. **Gold, Glory & Girls.** What do men want? What do they really want and need? This book takes them on a journey to the forth "G" that men need…GOD and the fulfillment that brings to their souls.

22. **I'm Praying The ROSARY for YOU!** This book will not only change your life as you pray the Rosary but will change the lives of family members and friends you pray for. You not only buy the book for yourself but buy a copy for each person you pray for and send them this personal book with their name written in it over 100 times! When a family member or friend read the prayers you are praying for them, they will, in many cases, be brought closer to God and begin to not only live out their faith, but begin to impact others too.

23. The Personalized ROSARY. You will learn how to pray the Rosary in a specific, purposeful, powerful way…just for YOU!   Your life will not be the same as you pray these prayers and draw closer to our Blessed Mother and Jesus Christ our Lord.

24. How To Pray The ROSARY For Your Family. You can have great impact on your family through your prayers. The Holy Spirit will take what you pray and in obvious and subtle ways make it happen in God's time as you pray specifically with purpose and direction. This book will guide you how to pray POWERFUL PRAYERS for your family, prayers that will not only change them…but you!

25. How To Be A MIGHTY MAN of GOD. In this book Dr. Young used the Scripture by St. Paul in I Corinthians 16:13-14 to develop the 5 STEPS that need to be taken to become a mighty man of God. This powerful book will awaken you of your need and move you to take simple steps to become the man you were always meant to be. It is a great book to use for a men's retreat with helps for leaders on how to organize one.

You can find other books written by Dr. Paul J. Young on:

DrPaulPress.com

This is a
TOTAL RELIEF *SYSTEMS*
publication

My prayer for you:

May you learn how to think and act in any situation
May you learn that you don't have to be weighed down by
>Hopelessness
>Anger
>Bitter
>Resentful
>Alone.

May you experience the fullness of who you were meant to be
>Bold
>Engaged
>Alive
>Filled with happiness
>Overflowing
>With exploding joy!

May God grant you the desires of your heart.

Amen

Be sure and read:

Dr. Paul's

TOTAL RELIEF Series

for depression, anxiety, etc.

You can find them at amazon.com

I would appreciate if you would **give me a good review of this book.** A good review (5 stars) encourages people to read the book and hopefully change their lives. Thank you for taking the time to do this. Go to this book title where you bought it at amazon.com.

A **DrPaulPress.com** publication

Products that make a difference now…and forever